The
Weekend
Landlord
(+ CD-ROM)

The
Weekend
Landlord
(+ CD-ROM)

From Credit Checks and Leases
to
GETTING PAID!

James A. Landon
Attorney at Law

SPHINX® PUBLISHING
AN IMPRINT OF SOURCEBOOKS, INC.®
NAPERVILLE, ILLINOIS
www.SphinxLegal.com

First Edition: 2005

Published by: Sphinx® Publishing, An Imprint of Sourcebooks, Inc.®

Naperville Office
P.O. Box 4410
Naperville, Illinois 60567-4410
630-961-3900
Fax: 630-961-2168
www.sourcebooks.com
www.SphinxLegal.com

This publication is designed to provide accurate and authoritative information in regard to the subject matter covered. It is sold with the understanding that the publisher is not engaged in rendering legal, accounting, or other professional service. If legal advice or other expert assistance is required, the services of a competent professional person should be sought.

From a Declaration of Principles Jointly Adopted by a Committee of the American Bar Association and a Committee of Publishers and Associations

This product is not a substitute for legal advice.

Disclaimer required by Texas statutes.

Library of Congress Cataloging-in-Publication Data
Landon, James A.
  The weekend landlord : from credit checks and leases to getting paid! / by James A. Landon.
      p. cm.
    ISBN 1-57248-477-2 (pbk. : alk. paper)
  1. Landlord and tenant--United States--Popular works. I. Title.
KF590.Z9L36 2005
346.7304'34--dc22
                                                                    2005005891

Printed and bound in the United States of America.
DR — 10 9 8 7 6 5 4 3 2 1

Acknowledgment

I would really like to thank my wife, Heidi, for providing the necessary moral support throughout this project. I would also like to thank Dan Bailey and Susan Labicane for providing initial insight and the type of constructive criticism that allowed the project to get off the ground.

Contents

How to Use
the CD-ROM

Thank you for purchasing *The Weekend Landlord*. We have worked hard to put together exactly what you need to get started as a landlord and to make sure that you are aware of some of the legal ramifications involved in your endeavor. We have also gathered what we believe to be some of the most important forms and documents you need to be successful. To make this material even more useful, we have included every document found in Appendix J on a CD-ROM that is attached to the inside back cover of the book.

Use the list at the end of this section for help finding the form you are looking for. You can use these forms just as you would the forms in the book. Print them out, fill them in, and use them however you need. You can also fill in the forms directly on your computer. Just identify the form you need, open it, click on the space where the information should go, and input your information. Customize each form for your particular needs. Use them over and over again.

The CD-ROM is compatible with both PC and Mac operating systems. (While it should work with either operating system, we cannot guarantee that it will work with your particular system and we cannot provide technical assistance.) To use the forms on your computer, you will need to use Acrobat® Reader®. The CD-ROM does not contain this program. You can download this program from Adobe's website at **www.adobe.com**. Click on the "Get Acrobat® Reader®" icon to begin the download process and follow the instructions.

Once you have Acrobat® Reader® installed, insert the CD-ROM into your computer. Double click on the icon representing the disc on your desktop or go through your hard drive to identify the drive that contains the disc and click on it.

Once opened, you will see the files contained on the CD-ROM listed as "Form #: [Form Title]." Open the file you need through Acrobat® Reader®. You may print the form to fill it out manually at this point, or your can use the "Hand Tool" and click on the appropriate line to fill it in using your computer.

Any time you see bracketed information [ ] on the form, you can click on it and delete the bracketed information from your final form. This information is only a reference guide to assist you in filling in the forms and should be removed from your final version. Once all your information is filled in, you can print your filled-in form.

NOTE: *Acrobat® Reader® does not allow you to save the PDF with the boxes filled in.*

. . . .

Purchasers of this book are granted a license to use the forms contained in it for their own personal use. By purchasing this book, you have also purchased a limited license to use all forms on the accompanying CD-ROM. The license limits you to personal use only and all other copyright laws must be adhered. No claim of copyright is made in any government form reproduced in the book or on the CD-ROM. You are free to modify the forms and tailor them to your specific situation.

The author and publisher have attempted to provide the most current and up-to-date information available. However, the courts, Congress, and your state's legislatures review, modify, and change laws on an ongoing basis, as well as create new laws from time to time. By the very nature of the information and due to the continual changes in our legal system, to be sure that you have the current and best information for your situation, you should consult a local attorney or research the current laws yourself.

. . . .

This publication is designed to provide accurate and authoritative information in regard to the subject matter covered. It is sold with the understanding that the publisher is not engaged in rendering legal, accounting, or other professional service. If legal advice or other expert assistance is required, the services of a competent professional person should be sought.

> —*From a Declaration of Principles Jointly Adopted by a Committee of the American Bar Association and a Committee of Publishers and Associations*

This product is not a substitute for legal advice.

> —*Disclaimer required by Texas statutes.*

Introduction

The chances are good that you have purchased this book for one of a variety of reasons. Maybe you have just purchased your first piece of investment property. Maybe you are simply contemplating such a purchase. Or maybe you have decided to rent out a room, or are moving into a bigger house and wish to keep your current residence rented as a source of supplemental income. Regardless of the reason, it is the intent of this book to provide you with an overview of the basic principles of residential landlord/tenant law in a format that is intended to be easy to read and understand, while covering a wide range of topics that may arise before, during, and even after a tenancy. With this knowledge, you will be in a much better position to accurately assess whether you and your current or future tenants are fulfilling your respective legal responsibilities.

The importance of a basic understanding of landlord/tenant law cannot be overstated. These laws can have a serious impact on the quality of your life. An uninformed or careless landlord may find him- or herself losing a significant amount of money or defending a lawsuit brought by a tenant. The primary goal of this book is not to turn you into a landlord/tenant law expert. That is not realistic and should not be your expectation. Rather, it is simply to educate landlords in the issues that they face every day, particularly those issues that lead to various landlord/tenant disputes.

The book is designed to give you the tools and knowledge to conduct yourself in a responsible and ethical fashion, while avoiding many of the pitfalls that residential landlords encounter. As a landlord, you should already know that important issues begin before a lease is signed. Such issues to consider include decisions on property management, advertising, credit applications, preparing a dwelling, etc. After the lease is signed, issues may arise regarding habitability of the unit, the responsibilities of both parties, maintenance, evictions, and hazardous conditions, just to name a few. Once the tenancy has been completed, issues often arise regarding the security deposit, suits for actual damages to the dwelling, and collection actions against former tenants. All of these aspects of a tenancy are addressed, and a series of forms and relevant state laws are attached for your convenience in the Appendices.

The material that follows covers the rental of a dwelling, which can include a home, apartment, mobile home, or other structure used as a sleeping place for one or more residents. This information only refers to property used as a residence. It does not refer to commercial property. This means that the following situations are not covered in this book.

- Residence at an institution, public or private, because of detention (jail) or the provision of medical, educational, counseling, or religious services (such as a mental hospital).
- Occupancy of a dwelling that you have a contract to purchase. If title is an issue between the parties, then by definition there is no legally recognizable landlord/tenant relationship.
- Occupancy by a member of a fraternal or social organization.
- Occupancy of a hotel/motel room.
- Occupancy by an employee of a landlord as a manager or custodian, whose right to occupancy is based on employment, such as a property manager.
- Occupancy of a mobile home space, if the tenant owns the mobile home and merely rents the space from the landlord. States generally have separate statutes dealing with tenants who are only renting a mobile home space, but own their own mobile home.

Chapter 1:

Before a Tenancy Begins

Any agreement involving the rental of another's residential real property involves three central components—a landlord, a tenant, and a rental agreement (also known as a lease). Residential real property refers to a house, apartment, condominium, mobile home, or any type of dwelling in which a tenant resides. The *landlord* rents the dwelling to the tenant, the *tenant* rents the dwelling from the landlord, and the *rental agreement* is the contract that binds both parties to each other through a series of terms and conditions.

Historically, landlord/tenant laws were heavily slanted in the landlord's favor, leaving tenants with minimal rights (if any). Our nation's history of lawmaking, known as the *common law*, had always shown a preference for landlord's rights, regardless of how unjust or oppressive those rights may have been. Tenants had little redress for problems caused by their landlords. Landlords knew their tenants were essentially powerless—no matter how neglectful the landlord may have been.

Change in this area came slowly, but it did eventually come. A slow but steady trend toward the recognition of tenants' rights emerged around the same time as the civil rights movement. In the early 1970s, reflecting this trend, the *Uniform Residential Landlord and Tenant Act* (URLTA) was drafted. This act laid the basic framework for many of our current landlord and tenant laws. It provided tenants with their first set of laws against landlords who rented substandard housing. Today, a number of states have adopted most or all of the language of URLTA as law.

States that have Adopted the URLTA

Alaska	Kansas	Oregon
Arizona	Kentucky	Rhode Island
Florida	Montana	South Carolina
Hawaii	Nebraska	Tennessee
Iowa	New Mexico	Virginia

With the continued emphasis on the expansion of tenants' right, it is expected that additional states will adopt the URLTA in the coming years. You can access the URLTA online at **www.lectlaw.com/files/lat03.htm**. If you live in a state yet to adopt the URLTA, it does not necessarily mean that your state's landlord/tenant laws are dramatically different. It just means that your state has not yet chosen to adopt the specific language contained within the Act.

Each state has its own landlord/tenant laws. While it is not possible to cover the specific procedural requirements for each state on issues like eviction procedures or exact time frames for notices in this one book, many of the laws affecting landlord/tenant relationships follow similar trends. Further, there are some federal laws that apply to landlords, no matter which state the property is located in. Those general landlord/tenant laws are discussed throughout this book.

Advertising

Since tenants do not grow on trees, landlords use a variety of forms of advertising to fill their vacancies. Typical forms of effective advertising include:

- ◆ word-of-mouth referrals from current tenants in other dwellings;
- ◆ advertisements in newspapers, local publications, apartment rental guides, movie theaters, online placement services, or television;
- ◆ distributing fliers in the neighborhood; and,
- ◆ placing a *for rent* sign either in the window or in the yard.

The particular type of advertising that may be appropriate for you can depend on who you are trying to attract, your budget, and your sense of urgency. No matter which form of advertising you choose, there are some simple rules that you should always follow when advertising a dwelling for rent.

Make sure your advertisement contains nothing discriminatory. You must always avoid discussions of gender, religion, race, disability, or *familial status*. (Familial status refers to marital status and families with children.)

Age should generally be avoided, although there is a small segment of housing devoted to senior citizens that is exempt from this type of discrimination claim. If there is any doubt as to whether your advertisement could be construed as discriminatory, contact a lawyer immediately. The potential penalties are too severe to ignore. The possible penalties include thousands of dollars in economic penalties, fines, or monetary awards levied against the property owner.

> **Landlord Tip**
> Make certain that your advertisement contains nothing discriminatory.

You also want to be realistic about the property that you have for rent. Be sure that your advertisement accurately portrays the state of the property. It is a waste of both your time and that of any prospective tenant to set up appointments and viewings for a property that does not fit a prospective tenant's need.

Use the advertisement as a *screening tool* to begin matching tenants to the type of property you have to offer. Do not be afraid to include in the advertisment the:

- ◆ rent;
- ◆ square footage;
- ◆ number of bedrooms and bathrooms;
- ◆ amenities;
- ◆ appliances and furnishings;
- ◆ general location;
- ◆ willingness to take pets; and,
- ◆ phone or email address for further information.

You may wish to omit other things that can be negotiated with the tenant, such as the length of the lease. It may be to your benefit to negotiate on this issue with the tenant. Your tenant may be willing to pay a higher monthly rent in exchange for a shorter lease. Conversely, you may be willing to offer a lower rent or a rental concession in exchange for a long-term lease.

> **Landlord Tip**
> Accurately describe the condition of the property in your advertising.

Rental Applications

When a prospective tenant is interested in a dwelling, a landlord's first step in dealing with this person should involve a *rental application*, also known as a credit application.

> **── Landlord Tip ──**
>
> A *rental concession* refers
> to a free period of rent in
> exchange for the tenant's
> promise to fulfill the terms
> of the lease. Under most rental
> concession provisions, the tenant
> will be required to pay back
> the value of the concession
> if the tenant does not fulfill
> the terms of the lease.

The residential credit application allows a landlord to evaluate the prospective tenant's income, prior rental history, employment, references, prior bankruptcies, criminal background, or any other item that the landlord can use to determine how *good* a tenant he or she may be, as well as his or her credit-worthiness. You will never know from a piece of paper whether you will have future problems with a tenant, but having some basic information about him or her can at least help you make an educated decision. Since the tenant's ability to pay is usually at the top of a landlord's criteria list, the tenant's credit-worthiness is very important.

Most landlords have some minimum financial criteria used to evaluate prospective tenants. For instance, a landlord may have a blanket rule that any prospective tenant will be refused if the basic monthly rent amount is over 28% of the prospective tenant's gross monthly income. Setting these guidelines not only helps a landlord evaluate applicants, it also demonstrates that a landlord is not accepting or rejecting prospective tenants on any arbitrary financial basis.

Landlords typically require certain information from a prospective tenant:
- full legal name;
- name of spouse, if any;
- date of birth;
- Social Security number;
- current address;
- previous addresses;
- employment;
- references;
- dependents;
- income;
- pet(s);
- bankruptcy history, if any;
- eviction history, if any; and,
- felony convictions, if any.

Be sure to have the prospective tenant fill out the application completely and accurately. It is well worth the few minutes it takes to confirm the information on the application to make sure that your prospective tenants do not have skeletons in their closets that make them a bad rental risk.

─Landlord Tip ─
A wise landlord will also request to see a picture identification from any prospective tenant.

The information provided by your prospective tenant is not irrelevant, and you should be diligent in evaluating each application. Beyond the applicant's name, you will obtain important information about the prospective tenant's current employer and employment history, prior addresses and landlords, banking information, references, and contact information. This information is not only useful in evaluating the credit application, but may also be useful at a later date (such as if the tenant has a balance due after the tenancy expires). The information on the credit application may help locate the tenant for *service of process* or provide information that can help pay an outstanding judgment. In evaluating a prospective tenant, information from previous landlords is especially important. Did the tenants fulfill the terms of their prior lease? Were they evicted? If a prospective tenant had problems with a previous landlord, why should you expect any different?

Credit Reports

On the rental application, you will need to include a statement that gives the landlord permission to contact references and to conduct a background check, as well as to run a credit check. This statement will serve as authorization or permission for you to receive the information you seek. These credit reports provide a wealth of valuable information and should be obtained for any new applicant. You can purchase a credit report from one of the following central credit reporting agencies.

Equifax
888-202-4025
(Sales)
800-685-5000
(Customer Service)
www.equifax.com

Experian
800-831-5614
www.experian.com

TransUnion
800-888-4213
www.transunion.com

The information contained in the credit report is invaluable. The credit reporting agencies are not advocates for your applicants. So, you will know that the information is an unbiased collection of personal, credit, and public record information.

Once you have chosen one of the credit reporting agencies, it is advisable to set up a business account. This may get you a lower rate per report ordered, and may cut the time it takes to get these reports.

Although the cost per report is minimal, you may recoup this expense from the applicant. Advise the applicant in advance (in writing) of the cost and obtain the applicant's consent to the charge—particularly if you intend the make the cost nonrefundable. Do not rely on the applicant getting the credit report or providing you with one. Even though they may argue that they can obtain one for free or just had one done, you want to keep control of this situation. While it is unlikely that most applicants will provide a false credit report, it is the tenant that you do not want who would.

Once the credit report has been obtained, you are looking to see that the information on the report matches the information provided on the application. Moreover, you should also be looking for information that is *not* on the application, such as prior bankruptcy information, child support orders, outstanding judgments, unpaid tax liens, or any other items that impacts the applicant's credit-worthiness, either in a positive or negative way.

In addition to the credit score, many credit reports will tell you:
- details about a prospective tenant's late bills;
- whether companies have *charged off* debt incurred by the prospective tenant;
- information relating to criminal convictions of the prospective tenant; and,
- past eviction actions against the prospective tenant.

If a prospective tenant provides any false or misleading information, you may use that fact to deny an application. If the information comes to light after the commencement of the tenancy, you can use it as a means of evicting the tenant.

Once the tenant's credit application is approved, the parties can move forward to the rental agreement or *lease*. If the credit application is denied, however, the tenant is entitled—by law—to an explanation. A landlord can lawfully reject an applicant for any of the following reasons:

> ─────── **Landlord Tip** ───────
> If a tenant's credit application is denied, he or she is entitled—by law—to an explanation.

- ◆ misrepresentations on the credit application;
- ◆ criminal background;
- ◆ poor credit history;
- ◆ insufficient income to pay rent;
- ◆ history of eviction; or,
- ◆ inability to meet the terms the landlord sets, such as an unauthorized pet.

These are all valid reasons for the rejection of an application. As long as you can document that one of these conditions exists, the denial of the application is not discriminatory. More importantly, it is unlikely that a court or other judicial entity would have any basis for a finding of discrimination.

It would be wise to provide a written letter of rejection, preventing any misunderstandings as to the specific reasons for denying the application. When providing a written rejection letter, be specific as to the reasons for the rejection. (You are more likely to get yourself into trouble by *sugarcoating* the specific reasons for the rejection.)

> ─────── **Landlord Tip** ───────
> When providing a written rejection letter, be specific as to the reasons for the rejection.

It is advisable to keep any letters of rejection and the denied applications on hand for a number of years. There is no hard and fast rule for the specific amount of time, but keep everything for at least five years. In the event that a disgruntled former applicant files a legal claim, you want to be able to demonstrate through your written documentation that nondiscriminatory grounds existed for the denial of the original application.

Do not allow a prospective tenant to move into a property before the credit application is approved and the lease or rental agreement has been signed. If you discover that the rental application does not warrant acceptance, you may be faced with the prospect of evicting the tenant. Do not take that chance. Provide the keys only after all relevant documentation is signed by both parties and upon your acceptance of the tenant's application.

Cosigners

If you are not convinced of a prospective tenant's ability to fulfill the terms of a lease, a cosigner may be required. The cosigner signs the rental agreement or lease, but does not actually reside in the dwelling. The primary function of the cosigner (from the landlord's perspective) is to guarantee payment to the landlord in the event that the tenant cannot make his or her payment. If the primary tenant is unable to fulfill the lease terms, the landlord will look to the cosigner for any rent or other damages that the tenant refuses or is unable to pay.

Cosigners are often required by landlords renting to college students who may not have any independent financial resources and have little credit history. If the cosigner appears financially able to pay the lease, there is little reason not to accept the applicant. The cosigner has a strong incentive to pay—not wanting to harm his or her own credit rating through any default of the tenant.

The cosigner should be required to sign both the credit application and the lease. The application should be signed so the landlord can confirm, via a credit check, that the cosigner indeed has the financial ability to pay in the event the tenant falters. Once a cosigner has signed the lease, he or she becomes jointly and severally liable for the tenant's obligation. This means that the cosigner is just as liable as the tenant and will have rights and remedies similar to the tenant. This also means that you should send all written notices for nonpayment not only to the tenant, but to the cosigner as well. Failure to do so may jeopardize your right to pursue a cosigner for any amounts contained in the notice.

─── Landlord Tip ───

It is advisable to look for a new applicant if a prospective tenant does not appear financially qualified and does not have a cosigner available.

Any *addendums* or modifications to the rental agreement should be signed by the cosigner as well as the tenant. (see p.21.) Without the cosigner's signature, you may be precluded from pursuing the cosigner for any amounts due based on the addendum or subsequent modification.

Fair Housing Considerations

Prior to the implementation of civil rights and fair housing legislation, landlords were often free to treat their tenants as they wished. This often translated into malicious and discriminatory behavior. Federal and state laws now prevent discriminatory practices specifically regarding housing. The federal *Civil Rights Act of 1968* prohibits discrimination for certain *protected classes of people*. The classes are based on race, color, religion, sex, national origin, or age. It is illegal to engage in any act that discriminates against a person of any protected class. The following illustrates situations for each protected class that would violate the 1968 act.

- ◆ *Race*—advertising that you encourage Caucasian applicants to keep the property safe from crime.
- ◆ *Color*—refusing to rent to Hispanic applicants because a former Hispanic tenant was always late with the rent.
- ◆ *Religion*—encouraging Christmas decorations, but discouraging Chanukah lights.
- ◆ *Sex*—rejecting a male applicant because you believe that females take better care of the property.
- ◆ *National origin*—denying an application solely because an applicant is not an American citizen.
- ◆ *Age*—encouraging older applicants in your advertising by stating that the apartment complex is known for its quiet environment.

The effort to prevent discrimination was further bolstered with the passage of the 1988 federal *Fair Housing Amendments Act* (FHAA). It expanded on the 1968 Act by forbidding discrimination against families with children or the handicapped. It is often referred to simply as the *Fair Housing Act*.

Protections for Those with Disabilities

The fair housing laws offer numerous additional protections for people with disabilities. This law pertains to all types of housing. One of the few exceptions is residences with four or fewer units, where the owner lives in one of the units. Under the FHAA, discrimination in renting a residence to anyone based on the covered protected classes is illegal.

The FHAA expands the traditional list of prohibited activities to actions that relate directly to discrimination based on disability.

─── **Landlord Tip** ───

Landlords should not:

- deny that a dwelling is available for rent if it is, in fact, available;
- refuse to rent to certain groups of prospective tenants;
- include limitations or preferences for certain types of tenants in advertisements;
- impose different terms and conditions for certain tenants; or,
- attempt to terminate a tenancy for a discriminatory reason.

In order to qualify for protection, a person must have an identifiable physical or mental disability, or some type of history of that disability. Unfortunately, it is difficult (if not impossible) to identify each and every condition that will qualify, particularly when considering mental disabilities. For instance, alcoholism and drug dependency are two characteristics that can lead to protection under fair housing laws. To make matters worse, asking a question designed to determine whether an applicant or anyone associated with that applicant has a disability is unlawful under FHAA. However, the Act does provide for certain inquiries, provided they are asked of all applicants whether or not they have a disability.

A landlord may ask:

- if an applicant can meet the financial requirements for the residence;
- if an applicant is eligible for housing that is available only to persons with a disability or a specific disability;
- if a person is eligible for a priority available only to persons with a disability or a specific disability;
- if a person is a *current* substance abuser; and,
- if an applicant has ever been convicted for the illegal manufacture or distribution of a controlled substance.

This leaves you in the dark as to whether additional protections for the tenant may be present. As a rule of thumb, if there is any question, assume that the current or prospective tenant qualifies as a person with a recognized and protected disability.

Landlords *must* permit reasonable modifications if such modifications are necessary for a disabled person to be able to live in and use the premises. The cost of the modification is to be paid by the disabled person. Modifications may be made to the interior of the individual's unit, as well as any public and common use areas of a building, including lobbies, hallways, and laundry rooms. These types of modifications may include installing appropriate ramps for the tenant's use or modifying a bathroom to meet the tenant's needs.

The landlord may reasonably set conditions for permission of any modifications of the property. Such conditions may include providing:

◆ a reasonable description of the proposed modifications;

◆ a reasonable assurance that the work will be done in a workmanlike manner with all applicable building permits being obtained; and,

◆ an agreement to restore the interior of the premises to the condition that existed before the modification (ordinary wear and tear excepted).

A landlord cannot increase any required security deposit because of the modifications. However, in some cases, to ensure that funds will be available for any necessary restoration at the end of the tenancy, the landlord may require the tenant to put money (not to exceed the cost of the restorations) into an interest-bearing *escrow account*. The interest earned on the account and any money left in it after the unit is restored to its original condition belongs to the tenant.

─── **Landlord Tip** ───

It is illegal for a landlord to refuse to allow a tenant with a disability to make modifications at the tenant's expense that would permit the tenant to fully enjoy the premises.

Not all modifications allow for this type of escrow account. Only modifications that need to be restored and are relatively expensive, qualify. Modifications, such as widening a bathroom door, that do not affect the usability of any other space and would not affect the next tenants' use of the residence, do not require restoration by the tenant. A modification, such as the removal of a cabinet under the kitchen sink, would require the tenant to restore the cabinet, as the next tenant may want the storage space under the sink. However, since the cost to replace one cabinet would not be tremendous, an escrow account would probably not be required. If the entire kitchen was redesigned, an escrow account may be required. A common situation in which an escrow account may be needed is when a tenant removes the bathtub and replaces it with a roll-in shower.

Remember, although a landlord may require that the tenant obtain permission to make modifications, the landlord cannot keep a disabled tenant from modifying the residence to meet his or her needs.

The FHAA also requires landlords to make reasonable modifications in rules, policies, practices, or services necessary to give persons with disabilities equal opportunity to use and enjoy the dwelling. Any policy or rule that denies a person with a disability access to a facility or service may be a violation of FHAA. Changes you may have to make include the following.

◆ Allow assistance animals. Disabled tenants may keep animals that assist them, such as guide dogs. However, the tenant is responsible for any damage or necessary cleaning as a result of the animal.

◆ Provide appropriate parking close to the tenant's dwelling.

◆ Allow for special arrangements regarding delivery of the rent or other fees due.

◆ Arrange for notices or other documents to be delivered in a manner suited for the tenant. (For example, a notice may have to be read to a blind tenant.)

Landlord Tip

Certain landlords may be exempt from discrimination claims based on the characteristics of their rentals. For example, owner-occupied dwellings with four or fewer units are exempt under the federal statutes, as are certain communities reserved for senior citizens.

A landlord does not have to allow every modification or accommodation requested. The law recognizes that landlords could be driven out of business if this were the case. A landlord does have the right to make sure that any request from the tenant is reasonable and appropriate, and the right to refuse requests that are not. If there is any question to the reasonableness of the request, the landlord should contact an attorney immediately for advice. These situations are too important for a landlord to leave to chance.

Unintentional Discrimination

It is important to remember that discrimination is not always overt—it may also be subtle. In fact, you may not even consciously realize that you are engaging in a form of discrimination. Some of the actions that a landlord may take that could ultimately lead to claims of discrimination include the following.

◆ Holding a Christmas party. The fact that the party is labeled as a Christmas party may offend some renters who feel that the party should be secular and nondenominational.

◆ Suggesting in your advertising that your community caters to a certain religious or ethnic group, or that the complex is looking for residents in a specific age range (unless the community is designated as one legally reserved for senior citizens).

◆ Requiring credit applications for some prospective applicants, but not for others.

The key to avoiding a discrimination claim is to treat everyone equally. This means that the application process should be the same for everyone—no exceptions.

Numerous states and municipalities have enacted their own fair housing laws as a supplement to the federal regulations. These local laws may or may not offer additional protections beyond the scope of the federal statutes. It is vitally important to understand that any party found to violate fair housing laws may be subject to severe penalties and fines.

Potential Penalties for Discrimination Claims

If you find yourself as a defendant in a discrimination case, the very first thing that you should do is contact an attorney with experience in landlord/tenant matters. The potential penalties in these cases are severe.

A judge may order compensation for actual damages—including pain, suffering, and humiliation—and can even force a landlord to make housing available to an aggrieved tenant. Insurance may or may not cover all of these expenses. For more information on your obligations regarding fair housing, contact your state's attorney general or the local Department of Housing and Urban Development (HUD) office. (Find more information about HUD at **www.hud.gov.**)

Chapter 2:

The Rental Agreement or Lease

The *rental agreement* or *lease* is the contract that binds the landlord and tenant together. While there is a slight distinction between the terms, they can typically be used interchangeably. (A lease indicates a written agreement for a lengthy period of time, whereas a rental agreement usually indicates a month-to-month agreement.) Some landlords like the security of a long-term lease, while others prefer the flexibility that a rental agreement provides. (It is much easier to terminate a month-to-month agreement.) The agreement may be either oral or written, but written agreements are always preferable. A written agreement is a contract the whole world can see, whereas an oral agreement is not.

With an oral rental agreement, the period is typically monthly. Unless the parties agree otherwise, the agreement automatically renews each month, until either party gives notice that he or she wants to terminate the obligation.

The length of a written agreement, on the other hand, varies widely. An agreement for a term means the written lease specifically states the length of a tenancy (which is often twelve months). There is no rule against a written month-to-month rental agreement. In fact, many landlords prefer these agreements, as they allow for a landlord to terminate if they so desire.

> **Landlord Tip**
>
> If you are considering a lease of more than one year, the *Statute of Frauds* dictates that your agreement must be in writing to be enforceable. (An oral rental agreement is only enforceable for one year or less.)

Terms of the Agreement

You and the tenant may include virtually any provision you would like in a written lease, as long as nothing violates the law or is *unconscionable*. An unconscionable provision is one that is so one-sided that it is oppressive and unfair to the other side.

Any residential lease should include certain provisions that are essential from a landlord's perspective. Those provisions include the following.

- *The names of the landlord and the tenant.* The names of both parties should be complete, and the tenant's Social Security number should be obtained, if possible. If the property is in the name of a trust or other corporate entity, the full name of that trust or corporate entity should be stated.
- *The physical address of the property.*
- *The length of the tenancy.* Specify whether the length is for a specific term or month-to-month. The length of the tenancy is a negotiable item between the parties, but the landlord should give some thought as to what would be the preferable term and negotiate from that point. For example, the landlord may want the flexibility of a month-to-month lease, but may be persuaded to accept a lease for one year in exchange for the tenant agreeing to a higher monthly rent.
- *The amount and nature of any security deposit.* It is imperative that your agreement spell out any nonrefundable portions of the deposit, as well as whether the tenant is paying first and/or last month's rent. (See Chapter 3 for further information on nonrefundable deposits and states that allow those types of deposits.) If your state allows nonrefundable deposits, they are generally a good idea—if only to ensure that some monies are available to clean the dwelling after the tenant moves out.
- *The amount of rent.* This figure should be listed per month. It is also often listed in the amount that will be paid over the term of the lease (if the lease is for a specific term).
- *The amount and calculation of late fees.* Late fees are generally calculated on a *flat fee basis* or on an *accruing basis* (usually by the day). Late fees accruing on a daily basis typically serve better as a means of persuading your tenants to pay the rent as soon as possible.
- *Any additional fees that are the tenant's responsibility.* You can propose that the tenant pay for all utilities, cable, parking, etc., or you can include these extra services as a part of a higher rent. If you choose to include additional services and make your rent all-inclusive, make

sure that you have budgeted appropriately in the rent that you are charging for these additional items. Otherwise, you may find yourself sacrificing a large part of the rent received.

◆ *The maintenance responsibilities of each of the parties.* While the landlord is responsible for supplying essential services that make the premises inhabitable, such as heating and running water, the parties can contract that the tenant be responsible for nonessential maintenance items, such as upkeep of the yard or swimming pool. You may find that you would be willing to reduce the rent in exchange for the tenant's commitment to these nonessential maintenance items.

◆ *The names of any additional occupants. Occupants* are those who live on the premises (such as children or a boyfriend) but are not named on the lease document. Accordingly, they do not have the rights of tenants. Keep this in mind.

◆ *The property is furnished or unfurnished, and if furnished, what furnishings are supplied.* Be specific as to the furnishings provided, including appliances, electronics, tools, supplies, and so on.

◆ *Any restrictions on the use of the property.* Make sure the property is not to be used for any purpose that is illegal or in violation of a local zoning ordinance.

◆ *The type of pets allowed.* If you allow pets, remember that even the best-behaved pets can cause damage. An additional pet deposit should always be required. This deposit should generally be nonrefundable (if allowed in your state).

◆ *A move-in/move-out inspection report.* These reports will prove very helpful in any later maintenance disputes and in claims regarding security deposit refunds.

◆ *The owner and/or property manager's address and telephone number.*

◆ *A clause that the prevailing party in any legal dispute is entitled to payment of his or her attorney's fees.* A judge may reject your request for attorney's fees if this clause is not present in your agreement.

◆ *A clause specifying if any move-in concession is being supplied to the tenant, and that the tenant is responsible for paying back the concession if he or she does not fulfill the terms of the lease.* A move-in concession is a fancy term for free rent, which you may give as an incentive to a new tenant.

◆ *The process of terminating the lease.* It should be spelled out that neither party can terminate unless in writing—no exceptions.

◆ *The signatures of all parties to the lease.*

Preprinted leases generally include most (if not all) of these provisions. However, preprinted leases usually only include the bare minimum of what should be included for each provision.

Do not be afraid to add important provisions to your lease. A blank standard lease is included in Appendix J. Any standard agreement will also have basic terms and conditions, also referred to as *boilerplate language*. These provisions include things such as the method of paying rent, calculation of late fees, security deposits, and default procedures. This standard language is included in virtually every written lease and includes provisions protecting both parties.

Oral Rental Agreements

If you are considering entering into an oral rental agreement, you are asking for trouble. No responsible landlord or tenant should ever enter into an oral rental agreement. First and foremost, an oral rental agreement demands that you have an extraordinary level of trust in the other party. Since you have no actual written document, the other party can simply claim that the agreement is not the same as what you know you agreed to. Maybe your tenant will announce that you agreed that he or she could have a pet in the dwelling. Or maybe he or she will announce that the agreed rent was to be $400 per month, when you set it at $500.

There are an infinite number of scenarios in which a landlord can be burned by the lack of a written lease. If you wind up in court with a tenant and you have no agreement, your right to a proper eviction is severely jeopardized. You have no proof of the amount of rent. The judge will probably deny your late fees and attorney's fees, since there is no lease supporting the award of these sums. It may be impossible to prove noncompliance, since there is no lease to examine. To avoid any of these potential problems, make sure your lease is in writing.

Liquidated Damages Provisions

A *liquidated damages provision* is a clause in the lease that requires the tenant to pay a set amount to the landlord for breaching the lease. An example would be a clause specifying that a tenant forfeits his or her entire security deposit if he or she leaves prior to the end of the lease.

These provisions are legal in some states, but illegal in others. Even in a state in which these provisions are illegal, however, the landlord always retains the right to pursue a tenant for actual damages. *Actual damages* is the term used to describe the actual monetary harm sustained by the landlord as a result of the tenant's breach.

Disclosures

The rental agreement should include a series of disclosures, some of which may be required by state law. These disclosures correspond to the blank spaces in the lease that need individual information. Disclosures can include the name and mailing address of the owner of the premises, the name of the person managing the premises on behalf of the owner, and the names of all tenants and occupants.

Blank spaces should be completed or marked "not applicable" or "N/A." *The rental agreement is not legally complete until every blank space contains the required information.* Once the rental agreement is completed, the landlord should keep the original and the tenant should be provided a copy, whether or not they request it.

Landlord Tip

It may be considered an act of noncompliance if the tenant fails to execute a fully filled out agreement to the landlord. It could also potentially be an act of noncompliance not to supply your tenant with a copy of that fully executed agreement.

Prohibited Provisions

Although the rental agreement is a voluntary contract, there are certain provisions that will not be allowed by law. Neither the landlord nor the tenant can legally waive federal or state rights or remedies that they would be otherwise entitled to have. A prime example would be the landlord's obligation to maintain the premises. The rental agreement cannot state that the landlord has no obligation to maintain the premises in a fit or habitable condition. Both court cases and state laws have mandated that landlords must keep the premises in a fit and habitable condition, and these cases and laws override any lease provision to the contrary.

Similarly, the rental agreement cannot excuse or limit a landlord's liability for any obligation created by law, nor can a tenant be required to *indemnify*, or protect, a landlord for any obligation created by law.

The rental agreement must also possess a certain level of fundamental fairness. If it places obligations only on the tenant that should be shared by both the tenant and landlord, the agreement could be discarded.

Example: *A clause stating that only a tenant would be responsible for attorney's fees in the event of court action would be unacceptable. Your provision should state that in the event of court action, the prevailing party will be entitled to his or her attorney's fees. A judge is likely to find that an attorney's fees provision is only enforceable if it goes both ways.*

If a provision in your lease is determined by a judge to be prohibited, the judge can strike the provision. This means removing the provision from the terms of the lease. The judge could also find that the entire lease agreement is null and void, thus depriving you of other rights you would have if the lease remained in effect. It is best to include a separate provision in your lease that states that any provision struck by the court will act as removing that provision only, and will have no effect on the remaining provisions of the lease.

Implied Provisions

Certain provisions will be implied in the lease, though not expressly written. An implied provision is one that is automatically and legally considered to be part of the lease. The courts are just as likely to enforce implied provisions as those expressly written into the agreement.

Examples of implied provisions include the following.

◆ The warranty of habitability, which requires that the landlord keep the premises to a minimum level of habitability, irrespective of what the rental agreement says.

◆ The landlord's duty to provide peaceful and quiet enjoyment of the premises.

◆ The rent due date is typically implied to be due on the 1st of each month, unless both parties agree otherwise.

◆ An expired tenancy that is not terminated is implied to be a month-to-month tenancy.

Changes to the Lease

Once a rental agreement has been signed by both parties and the tenancy has commenced, the rental agreement can still be changed. However, both parties must be willing to voluntarily alter or add provisions to the lease. To make such a change, you can use what is known as either an *addendum* or *subsequent modification*. Addendums or modifications are not applicable if only one party wishes to change terms—both parties need to be in agreement. Addendums or modifications are generally executed immediately after the lease is signed, or at a later date during the course of the tenancy. These often involve provisions not addressed in the lease, such as a tenant acquiring a pet two months after moving into the dwelling.

Any addendum or modification must be in writing—oral addendums or modifications are generally not valid. This is a peculiar aspect of landlord tenant law, since you may recall that a landlord and tenant may enter into a perfectly legal and valid oral rental agreement. However, if you want to ensure that an addendum will be enforceable, even if you only have an oral agreement, put any addendums or modifications in writing. Addendums and modifications should contain no additional terms beyond those that the parties intend to add or modify. As always, both parties should sign and date these documents, whether or not the lease is month-to-month or for a year.

Minors

The law generally states that contracts with minors are *voidable*. (*Minors* are people under the age of majority, which is 18 in most states.) This means that the there is a potential that the contract will not be enforceable against the minor. There are two exceptions to this rule. If a person under the age of majority is legally emancipated, then he or she may enter into contracts. *Legal emancipation* means that a court has rendered a decision that the minor will be afforded the same status as an adult and is legally on his or her own. The other exception is what the law calls *necessities*—things that are required for basic survival. In many court decisions, housing has been considered a necessity and minors have been ruled to be able to contract for such necessities. As a necessity, the minor will probably have to pay the prevailing market rate.

If possible, it is advisable that the landlord obtain the signature of a parent as cosigner. However, that option will often not be available. Minors may be legally emancipated, parents may be deceased, and so on. As long as the lease is in effect, the minor will be held to the same legal standards as any other resident.

Lease Expiration

When a lease expires, the parties have several options. Either party may terminate the lease, the parties may enter into a new lease for a specified term, or the parties may continue as they have, with the tenant continuing to pay the rent and the landlord continuing to accept it. For your tenants to properly terminate their obligation, they will need to vacate the rental unit on or before the final day of the lease and return the keys to you. If the keys have not been returned, your tenants have not legally relinquished possession.

If both parties wish to continue the lease but do not enter into any formal written agreement, there are still rules governing the continued tenancy. Both landlord and tenant are still bound by the original lease, with the exception that the lease has become a month-to-month tenancy in the vast majority of states. This may affect the procedure that either party must take to terminate the agreement. However, the provisions contained in the original lease do remain in effect during this month-to-month tenancy. When either party decides to terminate this month-to-month tenancy, he or she may do so according to the particular state's statutes.

If a tenant remains in a dwelling subsequent to the expiration of the lease, and no agreement is in place between the parties, the tenant is considered a wrongful *holdover*. This means that the tenant remains in possession of the dwelling without permission of the landlord. Many states allow a landlord to proceed quickly with the eviction process in this case. Do not collect rent from a tenant if the tenant remains in a dwelling after the expiration of the lease. If you accept rent, you may unwittingly be creating a month-to-month tenancy.

Chapter 3:

Security Deposits

A *security deposit* is technically defined as a certain amount of money deposited by a tenant with the landlord to assure the landlord of the tenant's full and faithful performance of the lease. In the real world, the deposit:

- ◆ compensates a landlord for unpaid rent, utilities, or other fees after a tenant moves out;
- ◆ is used to repair physical damage done to the unit during the course of the tenancy;
- ◆ pays for cleaning that may be necessary to put the dwelling in rentable condition after the tenant moves out; and,
- ◆ acts as an incentive to the tenant not to commit any damage and to keep the dwelling clean, so that he or she may recover all or a part of the deposit at a later date.

Some states do not address security deposits in their statutes, while others set limits on the amounts that a landlord can charge. It is important to remember that landlords ask for security deposits in every state. Every landlord should be aware of the penalties available to tenants in the event a court finds that a landlord has wrongfully withheld some or all of a tenant's deposit.

Wear and Tear

The security deposit is not prepaid rent. The purpose of the security deposit is to compensate the landlord for damages to a dwelling beyond *reasonable wear and tear*. A tenant's security deposit cannot be charged if the damages constitute normal wear and tear that would be expected during the course of a tenancy.

A landlord can charge a tenant for any damages beyond reasonable wear and tear, but those damages must have been caused by the tenant or the tenant's guests. For example, a tenant is not responsible for a window broken by a maintenance man.

Reasonable wear and tear is subjective, but is considered to be the wear and tear that would be expected based on the age and condition of the property, coupled with the length of the tenancy. For example, if a landlord installs brand new carpeting at the beginning of a tenancy, the landlord has a reasonable expectation that the carpeting should not have to be replaced within a year. This is not to say that all carpeting should be expected to last ten years, but it is probably a reasonable expectation that the new carpeting should last between five and ten years. If the tenant destroys the carpeting within a year, then the tenant will usually be responsible for most, if not all, of the recarpeting expense. However, if a tenant moves into a dwelling with nine-year-old carpeting, and the carpeting needs to be replaced after a year, it makes sense that the tenant will bear very little of the recarpeting costs, since the carpet was at the end of its useful life. From the example, it is easy to see that questions regarding reasonable wear and tear can become very subjective and must be reviewed on a case-by-case basis.

Refundable vs. Nonrefundable Deposits

A security deposit may be fully refundable, fully nonrefundable, or a combination of both. Refundable security deposits can be recouped by the tenant, while nonrefundable deposits remain with the landlord. The purpose of making a deposit nonrefundable is generally to ensure that the landlord has a certain amount of money to clean and redecorate the dwelling in advance of the next resident. If you live in a state that does allow for nonrefundable deposits, any nonrefundable security, cleaning, or redecorating deposit should be clearly and explicitly stated in the rental agreement. The cleaning and redecorating deposit is required for the landlord to make the dwelling presentable to future tenants once the current tenancy terminates.

Deposits will be presumed refundable unless it is worded in the rental agreement that the deposit, or a specific portion of it, is nonrefundable. If you happen to live in one of the relatively few states that allow these nonrefundable deposits, it is advisable that the landlord require a nonrefundable deposit, if for nothing else than to ensure that some monies are available for cleaning and redecorating once the tenancy has expired.

However, always be mindful of the restrictions that your state may place on the overall deposit that you can require of any new tenant. Even if your state allows a nonrefundable deposit, market forces may preclude you from seeking such a deposit. For instance, you may feel the need to increase your occupancy rate, and none of the other landlords in your area require such a deposit. In such cases, nonrefundable deposits may be impractical.

The following states have statutes allowing certain nonrefundable deposits.
   ◆ Arizona
   ◆ Florida
   ◆ Georgia
   ◆ Nevada
   ◆ New Jersey
   ◆ North Carolina
   ◆ Oregon
   ◆ Utah
   ◆ Washington
   ◆ Wisconsin
   ◆ Wyoming

Move-In Inspection

One of the most important steps in renting a dwelling involves the move-in inspection form. It will be a factor in determining what is charged up front as a security deposit and will be critical as a comparison to the condition of the space after the tenancy ends to determine what charges are made against the security deposit.

It is the opportunity for a tenant to document every item within the home that needs the landlord's attention prior to moving in. It is also your opportunity to discover the items that need to be immediately addressed. Without this inspection, it can be difficult to determine whether a problem occurred prior to, during, or even after the tenancy. Consequently, your tenant should not move in until this inspection is complete.

A move-in inspection should be in written form, addressing various aspects of the dwelling, and should include the following general categories:

- living room or den areas;
- kitchen;
- dining area;
- each bedroom;
- each bathroom;
- front and rear yard;
- swimming pool or hot tub, if applicable;
- basement, if applicable;
- heating and cooling system;
- appliances;
- furnishings provided by the landlord;
- light fixtures in each room;
- doors in each room;
- condition of floors, walls, and ceilings in each room; and,
- garage, if applicable.

Remind your tenants that they should not just give a cursory inspection of the premises. Each room should be thoroughly inspected. (If your tenants are savvy, pictures or videotape will be taken.)

It is to your benefit to give each tenant a form to complete. You need to take appropriate action when deficiencies are brought to your attention. If you ignore any deficiencies, your tenants may be able to claim that you are in breach and may possibly terminate the tenancy. The form provided to the tenants does not need to be overly complicated, but should include the general categories outlined. The tenants should be able to provide an answer in an appropriate space for each category, noting the current condition, and if subpar, what they believe is the appropriate remedy.

Appropriate Deposit

The appropriate deposit for your rental depends on a few factors.

- *The allocation of the deposit between refundable and nonrefundable portions.* A higher nonrefundable deposit means that you may ask for a higher deposit overall, subject to any maximum deposit allowed by your state.

- *The amount of the monthly rent.* It just makes sense that a dwelling calling for a higher monthly rent will call for a higher security deposit.
- *The rental market in your area.* The economic realities of high vacancy rates may persuade you to allow tenants a reduction in the security deposit.
- *The condition of the dwelling.* An appropriate deposit for a fixer-upper is probably quite a bit less than for a pristine property.
- *Your state statutes.* Some states limit the amount of security a landlord can legally request.

Accounting for Deposits

When a tenant moves out, you have an obligation to account for the tenant's security and other deposits. This is accomplished through a security deposit statement, which is a written record of the tenant's deposits, followed by the landlord's explanation of all deductions from that deposit. This form should be completed for all residents upon moving out and should include detailed itemization of the deductions.

You may encounter a situation where your state requires a security deposit statement before you have completed the cleaning and repair process. In this event, make sure that you still send a security deposit statement to your former tenant in a timely fashion. The statement should reflect that final deductions have yet to be determined, but that a final statement will be sent as soon as those final deductions can be properly itemized. This allows you to prevent running afoul of any state statute giving tenants the right to seek damages for the security deposit statement not sent in a timely fashion.

You may also live in a state that requires deposits to be placed into an interest-bearing account for the tenant. Each state that requires deposits be put into an interest-bearing account has its own rules for when it is necessary. Following is a list of states that require landlords to keep deposits in an interest-bearing account under certain situations. If your state appears, you will need to do some additional research to learn the exact requirements for your state.

> **States that Require Landlords to Pay some Form of Interest on Deposits**
>
> | | |
> |---|---|
> | Connecticut | New Hampshire |
> | District of Columbia | New Jersey |
> | Florida | New Mexico |
> | Illinois | New York |
> | Iowa | North Dakota |
> | Maryland | Ohio |
> | Massachusetts | Pennsylvania |
> | Minnesota | Virginia |

Deposits Wrongfully Withheld

What happens if a landlord fails to provide a security deposit statement including monies that may be due to the tenant? Under both URLTA and various state laws, if a landlord fails to properly account for a deposit in a timely manner, the tenant may recover damages from the landlord. These damages generally consist of any money wrongfully withheld by the landlord. Wrongfully withheld funds are those kept by the landlord that should have been returned to the tenant. If a tenant files suit against a landlord claiming that all or part of the deposit has been wrongfully withheld, many jurisdictions allow damages in addition to any deposit deemed wrongfully withheld. In Arizona, for example, state statutes allow a tenant to recover twice the amount of any wrongfully withheld deposit from a wrongdoing landlord, plus interest from the date that the money should have been returned to the tenant.

> **Landlord Tip**
>
> Many tenants (and some landlords) are under the mistaken belief that the security deposit can be used as the last month's rent. That is not true.

It is up to the tenant to prove to the court that a landlord has wrongfully appropriated funds. Be mindful that the landlord does not need to have intentionally withheld funds inappropriately. It is a matter for the court to determine that the landlord should have returned those funds.

Since these damages can be steep, a responsible landlord will ensure that all security deposit statements are sent out in a timely manner, even if the landlord believes that the tenant is not entitled to any refund.

The deposit should not be used as the last month's rent nor should even a part of it. The deposit is designed to allow you to make necessary repairs to put your property back to a rentable condition after your tenant vacates. If you allow the deposit to be used for rent, you are preventing yourself from having funds to make those necessary repairs. The law is firmly on your side on this subject. Rent is rent; the deposit is the deposit; and, the tenant has no right to direct the landlord to use the deposit in any other way.

Property Sold During the Tenancy

Properties often change hands during the course of a tenancy. If the landlord sells the property during the course of the tenancy, the security deposit can be returned to the tenant or transferred to the new owner. The buyer and seller of the property should agree prior to closing whether the security deposit will be returned to the tenant or transferred to the new owner. If the deposit is not returned to the tenant, the law considers the owner of the property at termination of the tenancy to be the responsible party in any security deposit dispute. Therefore, it is imperative for landlords to promptly notify tenants of any change in ownership. The new owner will ensure that the tenants know where to send the rent and whom to call in the event of any maintenance issues. The former owner will alleviate the risk of any suit being brought for a security deposit dispute, which becomes the responsibility of the new owner.

Chapter 4:

Rent

As a landlord, your primary focus is presumably on the collection of rent. However, a multitude of factors are at play in any landlord's desire to obtain the maximum amount of rent in an efficient and organized manner. The quality of the property, the square footage, number of bedrooms and bathrooms, included amenities, area of town, and the current rent for similar properties are just some of the factors that determine the appropriate asking price for your rental property.

If you are a new landlord, do not hesitate to visit properties in your area and find out the amount of rent the other properties are charging. Take note of the amenities included with these properties. Are they offering a rental concession or free utilities? Are additional services, such as workout facilities, available on the premises? You may need to consider offering services that you did not previously consider. Remember, these other properties are competing for available tenants, and any information you can obtain makes it easier to determine the best route to finding tenants that maximize your rental income while minimizing the time that your rentals stay vacant.

Rent Control

There are only a handful of states or cities with restrictions on the amount of rent a landlord can legally charge. These areas include parts of California, Maryland, New Jersey, New York, and the District of Columbia. If you are not in an area with *rent control*, you may price the rent as you see fit. If you do live in a rent-controlled area, laws may limit the amount of rent you may charge, your ability to raise the rent, and even eviction procedures. If you do live in a rent-controlled area, do your best to familiarize yourself with your local rent control ordinances.

If you own rental property not subject to rent control, there is no prohibition on the amount of rent. However, as a practical matter, it does not mean that you can charge whatever you want. Market forces will inevitably create a ceiling on your rent. On the whole, you are much better off than landlords subject to rent control.

Receipts for Rent

When the rent or other charges are paid, a receipt should be given showing the date, time, and amount paid. Receipts should be given on a consistent basis. You always want a paper trail documenting all money received. This is especially true if a tenant claims to have paid but cannot produce a receipt. If you give receipts every time you receive money, you can simply say that the tenant must be mistaken. However, if you only give receipts on a spotty basis, your claim that the tenant must be mistaken carries much less weight in a court of law.

┌──Landlord Tip──┐
Do not accept cash unless absolutely necessary, as cash does not leave a paper trail.

If you accept cash, a receipt is a must. It is proof of payment for both yourself and the tenant. Checks or money orders both leave a paper trail. Lost checks and money orders can be traced, whereas cash cannot.

Drop Boxes

You may have a drop box available for your tenant's convenience, which theoretically allows rent to be paid at any hour of the day or night. While this sounds good in theory, the use of a drop box is discouraged under most circumstances. With a drop box, the tenant receives no receipt and the drop box may be located in a place vulnerable to theft. Plus, the use of a drop box can lead to disputes regarding if rent has been paid and when the payment was made.

It is very easy for a tenant to claim that the payment was dropped in the box after hours, and then the landlord was not able to find any such payment. Although the tenant may be certain that the payment was left in the drop box, there is no verifiable proof that the landlord actually received the rent.

As a general rule, only accept payments given directly to you or a property manager, or those sent by mail. Accepting payments by mail is not as foolproof as direct payments, but is definitely preferable to a drop box. If using mail, you may instruct your tenants to send the rent to a physical address, typically either your home or office address. Many landlords prefer to receive rent through a post office box.

Nonpayment of Rent

When a tenant has not paid rent in a timely manner, a landlord may give a *notice of nonpayment of rent*, also known as a *pay or quit notice*. In all but a handful of states, this notice may be given to the tenant on the day after the rent is due, or any day thereafter. (Connecticut, Delaware, Maine, Oregon, and Rhode Island provide varying short grace periods before a notice may be given.)

Unless otherwise specified, rent is typically due on the first day of the month. If you own multiple rentals, the first day of the month is a logical day, as it creates uniformity for all of your rentals. The only situation in which rent is not due on the first is if the parties have specified in the lease that rent is due on another specific day of the month. Even if the first falls on a weekend or holiday, your tenant is still generally responsible for submitting the rent by the due date. Do not just assume that your tenants will be cognizant of this fact. Remind them, if necessary.

The nonpayment of rent notice should include the tenant's name and address, date, and the amount and calculation of all fees charged to the tenant. The notice should also specify that court action will follow if the tenant does not pay the amount due within the time frame contained in the notice. This notice cannot legally be given either before or on the date that the rent is due, as rent is not considered late until the day after it is due. Once that date passes, however, the nonpayment of rent notice can be given at any time.

A notice for nonpayment of rent (as well as other notices delivered to your tenant) should be delivered by hand, or alternatively, by certified mail. Do not post the notice on the door or in another place where you believe the tenant will find it. This is not an acceptable method of delivery.

Amount and Calculation of Late Fees

Late fees are typically calculated in one of two ways—either on a daily basis or as a flat fee. The calculation of your late fees should be included in your lease or rental agreement, and you can only collect what is specified in that written agreement. Include a provision in the lease that states that late fees continue to accrue on a daily basis. This gives your tenants a greater incentive to pay as soon as they are able, so the fees do not continue to accrue. That same motivation may not be present with a flat late fee.

As a general rule, the amount of late fees charged to the tenant must be reasonable. Two dollars ($2) per day on a $1,500 per month rental house is likely to be reasonable. Two hundred dollars ($200) per day is not.

If a court finds that the amount of your late fees are unreasonable, it may limit your claim to them. This limit could be the amount that the judge finds to be reasonable, or the court may find that the late fee provision of the lease is unconscionable as a matter of law and is therefore unenforceable. If that happens, you would collect no late fees. A provision is *unconscionable* if the judge believes that it is simply unreasonable to impose on the tenant.

It is important to remember that the landlord's right to collect late fees in a court of law often requires that the fees be specified in writing. If you only have an oral rental agreement, it is doubtful that a judge will enforce any late fee on the tenant. (This is another reason that all of your leases or rental agreements should be in writing.)

Other Fees

The parties can agree that the tenant is responsible for paying a variety of other fees, including utilities—such as water, gas, or electricity—and things like cable television or parking fees. These fees need to be spelled out in the lease, and like late fees, should always be reasonable. Unreasonable fees are likely to be unenforceable fees.

Partial Payments

In many places, a landlord can legally refuse to accept a partial payment of rent and other charges, but cannot refuse an offer of payment in full (unless the tenant is in the midst of a notice for noncompliance unrelated to the rent). If you accept partial payments, do not assume that you can accept them without consequences. Indeed, landlords in many places waive their rights if partial payment is accepted without a signed agreement documenting the date upon which the balance is due.

The proper way to handle partial payments involves a document called a *partial payment agreement*. Have the tenant sign the document at the time that the payment is accepted. It details the amount received by the landlord, as well as the date(s) upon which the balance of rent and other fees will be paid. If the tenant refuses to sign the agreement, refuse to accept the partial payment. Without this document, you may be barred from proceeding with eviction for the remainder of that month. (See Appendix J for a form partial payment agreement.)

Insufficient Funds Checks

Landlords have the right to charge an additional fee if a check bounces, but that fee must be outlined in writing to the tenant before it will be enforceable. If no provision is present in your current lease, add a provision for future leases that allows you to collect a set fee per bounced check. In order to provide the proper incentive, the bounced check fee should be no less than $25.00. If no provision for a bounced check fee is present in your lease, you cannot collect additional penalties from your tenant. However, your state may allow prosecution for repeated bounced checks. Call your local district attorney's office for further information.

> **— Landlord Tip —**
> If you receive one bad check from your tenant, you do not have to risk it happening a second time. Require from that point forward that your tenant pay you in certified funds, such as a money order or cashier's check.

Raising the Rent

You cannot simply raise the rent unless you have a legal right to do so, and then only with a valid notice. Both parties are bound by the amount of rent stated in the rental agreement. However, you can raise the rent:

◆ when the term of the lease expires and

◆ under an appropriate state statute, giving proper notice that the rent due on a month-to-month agreement will be increased.

The landlord is required to disclose, in writing, the new amount of rent to be paid and the effective date of the rent increase. If the parties reach the end of a term for a lease, and neither party takes any action, the lease is presumed to continue upon the same terms as before. In other words, all pertinent provisions remain the same, including the amount of the monthly rent.

Chapter 5:

The Landlord's Duties

Landlords face many continuing duties after the rental agreement has been signed, sealed, and delivered. Some of these duties come from ancient court decisions, while some come from more recent decisions. Any of these court-made laws are known as the *common law*. Other duties the landlord is responsible for come from state or federal statutes, or from local housing ordinances. There are also duties imposed on the landlord by the agreement he or she made with the tenant. These obligations are discussed in this chapter.

Duty to Deliver Possession to Tenant

Once a rental agreement or lease has been signed by both parties, the landlord's first obligation is to make sure that the tenant can actually move in. This may sound strange, but it is not all that uncommon for landlords to find unauthorized people living in their property. If this occurs, the landlord can bring an eviction action against the unauthorized occupants (if the police will not remove them as trespassers). The tenant does not have the obligation to pay rent until possession of the property is with the tenant. If the landlord's failure to deliver possession is found to be intentional or in bad faith, the tenant may be able to recover damages.

Duty to Maintain Fit Premises

As a result of numerous state laws and court decisions, landlords now have an obligation to keep the premises in a fit and habitable condition. This is also referred to as the landlord's *implied warranty of habitability*. This means the landlord shall:

◆ comply with any applicable building codes affecting health and safety;

◆ make all repairs necessary to keep the premises fit and habitable;

◆ keep all common areas of the premises in a clean and safe condition;

◆ maintain, in good and safe working order and condition, all electrical, plumbing, sanitary, heating, ventilating, and air conditioning, as well as other facilities and appliances—including elevators;

◆ provide and maintain receptacles for the removal of ashes, garbage, rubbish, and other waste incidental to the occupancy of the dwelling, and arrange for their removal;

◆ supply running water and reasonable amounts of hot water at all times; and,

◆ provide reasonable heat and air conditioning or cooling where such units are installed and offered, except in places where the dwelling is not required by law to be equipped for those purposes, or instances in which the heat or cooling is generated by an installation within the exclusive control of the tenant and supplied by a direct utility connection.

What does all of that mean? In layman's terms, it means that the landlord has an ongoing obligation to keep all essential services in good working order. If this does not happen, a tenant can terminate a tenancy and possibly recover damages from the landlord. Far too many landlords ignore this obligation and find themselves regretting that decision when they appear in front of a judge.

In order to maintain the premises, the landlord must have a system for maintenance and repair. All tenants should have a working phone number for the landlord and the person in charge of maintenance. The landlord's file should include written requests for maintenance and repair received from the tenant.

Virtually every state has adopted the concept of this implied warranty of habitability to one extent or another. Even in the few states that have not, local housing ordinances are likely to provide specific health and safety requirements of landlords, which essentially provide the same protection to tenants.

The only situation in which the duty to maintain the premises may be abated is in the event that the tenant is responsible for causing the problem. In that event, the tenant may be forced to bear the responsibility of paying for the repair or restoration of the required service. Otherwise, the reason for any disruption in an essential service is the responsibility, both legally and financially, of the landlord.

If you find yourself unsure of your responsibilities, particularly if you are concerned that your rentals may be considered uninhabitable, numerous resources are available at your disposal. For general housing information, contact your state's attorney general, the Department of Housing and Urban Development (HUD), your local fair housing authority, or your state's department of real estate. Chances are also good that a local or state landlord's advocacy group is available for questions, including basic interpretations of your state's landlord/tenant laws.

> **Landlord Tip**
>
> If your rental property contains a swimming pool, you need to provide adequate protection for your tenants. Appropriate fencing around the pool is a must, as are posted signs concerning the need to supervise young children, hours in which the pool may be used (if appropriate), and a caution regarding the slippery nature of a pool deck.

Your Tenant's Right to Withhold Rent

As landlord/tenant laws slowly evolve, state statutes have given tenants an ever-expanding array of rights in the event that a landlord is shirking his or her responsibilities toward habitability. The right to withhold rent, or in the alternative, to make the repairs and deduct the cost from the rent, is among this new class of rights available to tenants across the country. Before a tenant can invoke this right, however, one of several requirements must be present.

◆ The tenant (or his or her guests) cannot be responsible for the problem.

◆ The repairs necessary must be the result of problems that are material in nature. In other words, the problem must be of a sufficient nature.

◆ The landlord has been notified of the problem in writing and has failed to remedy the situation.

Oral notices are unlikely to be upheld in a court of law, but do not ignore written notices from your tenants. In the event that you receive written notice from your tenant threatening to withhold rent, do not hesitate to inspect the dwelling to confirm that the problem exists. If it does, do not hesitate in your efforts to effectuate repairs. Your tenants may be able to claim damages in the event that you are nonresponsive to a valid request for repairs. Some states permit tenants to withhold rent and allow tenants to repair minor problems and deduct the cost from their rent.

Dangerous Conditions and Waste

If a tenant has knowledge of a condition that is threatening the premises or creating a chance for injury, such as a hole in the ground that might not be easily visible, the tenant has a duty to inform the landlord of the condition. The tenant may become personally liable for failing to inform the landlord of the problem in a timely fashion (if, for example, the problem was only known to the tenant).

Likewise, a tenant has a duty not to commit waste during the course of the lease. This means that the tenant cannot let the property fall into a state of disrepair as a result of his or her tenancy. If this occurs, the tenant can be held liable for actual damage to the rental unit that occurred during the course of the tenancy, including potential damages for the reduction in the value of the property. A landlord can pursue those damages via a lawsuit filed subsequent to the tenancy, after the landlord has regained possession of the premises. Once the landlord regains possession of the premises, he or she is in position to ascertain the exact amount of damages to the property and the dollar amount necessary to return the property to a rentable condition.

Hazardous Conditions

The presence of hazardous conditions on your property can potentially be one of the most serious issues facing landlords, particularly as rental housing ages. Different building materials were used in the past, and only recently has the harmful nature of a variety of these building materials become known. The prime examples of hazardous conditions seen in rental property include:

- ◆ lead-based paint;
- ◆ asbestos;
- ◆ mold;
- ◆ carbon monoxide; and,
- ◆ radon.

Lead-Based Paints

Residential property built prior to 1978 is likely to contain lead-based paint. Lead is known to pose a health risk to the population, with prolonged exposure leading to lead poisoning.

The federal government has enacted requirements mandating that landlords disclose information on lead-based paints to prospective tenants if the property was built before 1978. If you would like more information on lead-based paints in your area, contact your local housing authority or environmental protection agency.

When you sign an agreement with a new tenant, you will need to disclose the presence (or lack thereof) of any lead-based paint on the dwelling. This should be done with a lead-based paint disclosure form. (Use the disclosure form in Appendix J.)

Further information about the hazards associated with lead-based paints can be obtained online at the following address.

www.homebuying.about.com/cs/leadpaint/a/leadpaintfacts.htm

Asbestos

Asbestos has long been linked with cancer. When exposed, asbestos fibers are released into the air and are easily inhaled. Asbestos often becomes exposed during renovation or repair work conducted on the property. If you believe that asbestos has been exposed, contact appropriate experts to conduct the removal of any hazardous material immediately. Do not attempt to remedy the problem yourself. You can obtain asbestos testing information, including information on local testing resources, by calling EMSL Analytical, Inc. at 800-220-3675.

The presence of asbestos is a source of potential liability. If you want to responsibly respond to the problem, here are some suggestions.

◆ If you believe asbestos to be present in the dwelling, do not disturb it. Immediately seek help from a licensed expert.

◆ Regularly inspect your property if you believe that the age of the property would indicate the presence of asbestos (approximately pre-1980).

◆ Immediately inform your residents if the presence of asbestos is confirmed.

A valuable website for further information on the hazards and remedies associated with asbestos is the environmental protection agency at **www.epa.gov/asbestos**.

Mold

The presence of mold seems to be a fairly new phenomenon, but it is catching on quick. Mold thrives in humidity and water. It can quickly spread throughout walls, ceilings, and on paint. However, since mold is primarily fueled by moisture, the age of a dwelling has little to do with the likelihood of developing mold, and the landlord will not always be liable for its presence. The most efficient ways for a landlord to deal with mold include:

- ◆ regular inspections of the property, particularly if you live in a humid, damp environment;
- ◆ educating your tenants about the dangers of mold, and implore them to report any signs as soon as is practicable; and,
- ◆ remediating the problem as soon as the evidence of mold is confirmed.

Remember, mold is not an occurrence that depends on the age of the property. It is not unreasonable for a landlord to not know about a growing mold problem, even if he or she responsibly checks for such a problem. You will only incur liability for not maintaining or correcting a problem that you know or should know about. If the tenant neglects to inform you of the mold's presence, you are unlikely to be found responsible.

Information about the danger of mold can be found online at **www.mold-help.org**, and remediation information can be found from the National Center for Environmental Health at 888-232-6789.

Carbon Monoxide

Carbon monoxide is produced not only by automobiles, but within home appliances that involve fuel, such as water heaters, furnaces, fireplaces, grills, and stoves. Carbon monoxide can quickly overcome a resident and can easily result in death. In order to avoid potential liability, here are some commonsense procedures to follow.

- ◆ Regularly inspect appliances that burn fuel for any obvious blockages.
- ◆ Regularly inspect any pilot lights for irregularities.
- ◆ Regularly inspect and maintain all smoke detection and carbon monoxide detection devices.

In the event that an injury occurs as a result of carbon monoxide poisoning, the responsibility falls on the party responsible for the problem. Landlords are generally responsible, unless the parties have shifted responsibility for maintenance to the tenant, or the tenant is clearly at fault for intentional or obviously negligent behavior. Unfortunately, it is difficult for landlords to legally reject any responsibility, unless the tenant refuses access for the landlord to inspect the property.

For telephone inquiries, contact the Environmental Protection Agency at 202-272-0167. Further information on the dangers of carbon monoxide can be found at two informative websites:

www.epa.gov/iaq/co.html
and
www.carbonmonoxidekills.com.

Radon

Radon is a radioactive gas that naturally occurs around areas of uranium soil or rock. Radon begins to cause particular problems with older dwellings, as these dwellings tend to have poor ventilation. Radon has the potential to cause lung cancer with prolonged exposure. If there is any reason to believe that radon gas may be present, purchase and maintain a test kit, and immediately provide enhanced ventilation if necessary. If you live in a state in which radon is a concern, include a clause in your lease regarding the radon risk. The clause may read something like the following.

> *RADON GAS: Radon gas is a naturally occurring radioactive gas that can present health risks to people over time if accumulated in sufficient quantities.*

Further information regarding radon and radon testing, including whether radon gas is considered to be a problem in your area, may be obtained from county, state, or federal housing authorities. Another valuable resource for testing information is **www.radon.com**. A quality resource for general information is **www.epa.gov/radon**. The Environmental Protection Agency has an indoor air quality clearinghouse at 800-438-4318 that can help with individual state resources on radon.

Smoke Detectors

Many jurisdictions now require the use of working smoke detectors in rental property. However, this is an area in which you should not wait on your jurisdiction to require such a detector. If no working smoke detector is installed in your rental property, install one in each and every unit, immediately. These detectors not only save lives—they potentially save landlords from the liability generated when a detector should be present, but is not.

Older Structures

Housing codes and ordinances around the country often exempt certain buildings and structures from the housing enforcement codes. A piece of property exempted from the codes is known as *grandfathered*. This means that property built before a specific date will not necessarily be subject to the same codes or regulations that are effective for newer properties. If you are uncertain as to whether your rental property may be grandfathered from certain responsibilities, contact your local municipal housing authority. Decisions about grandfathered properties are generally going to be made on a local level. However, certain obligations—particularly those relating to cooling, heating, hot water, and other essential services—will be required regardless of the age of the property.

> **Landlord Tip**
>
> Even if you own property grandfathered from certain responsibilities, never ignore your obligation to provide cooling, heating, hot water, or any other service deemed essential under your state's landlord and tenant laws. These responsibilities can never be ignored, no matter how old your property may be.

Peaceful and Quiet Enjoyment of the Premises

The landlord's duty to provide peaceful and quiet enjoyment, commonly called a *covenant of quiet enjoyment*, is the landlord's promise that the tenant will not be disturbed by any third party. In other words, the landlord is assuring the tenant that, during the entire course of the tenancy, the tenant will enjoy full and undisturbed use of the property.

The duty, which is implied (even if not expressly contained in your lease), may not initially seem important, but is actually a critical component of the landlord's responsibility to the tenant. As with any other breach of the lease by the landlord, the tenant may be able to terminate the lease and possibly recover damages if a judge believes that the landlord has violated this basic duty.

Landlord's Right of Access

Once a tenant has been given the keys to the rental property, through the time that the tenant returns those keys or an eviction proceeding is complete, specific rules govern the landlord's right of entry into the rental property. Although a tenant has a reasonable expectation of privacy in his or her dwelling, the landlord does retain a right to access the premises, provided that the landlord follows the state-specific rules of entry.

Under extraordinary circumstances, the landlord has a right to gain immediate access if a true emergency exists, such as a fire, flood, or the presence of some other imminent emergency. If a true emergency does not exist, a landlord may only gain access if proper notice has been given to a tenant, and a reasonable amount of time passes between the notice and the landlord's entry.

States have come to different conclusions as to the amount of time required for a proper notice, but the most common time frame is between twenty-four and forty-eight hours. The landlord should give written notice of the intent to enter the premises, and the entry should only be at reasonable times, such as during normal business hours. (A notice of landlord's intent to enter the premises is included in Appendix J.)

The landlord cannot and should not enter a dwelling without reason. Repeated entries without cause, even if proper notice has been given, will likely lead to claims of harassment. Conversely, a tenant cannot refuse legitimate access to the dwelling. If a tenant refuses to allow lawful access, a landlord may send the tenant a written notice of noncompliance. Eventually a landlord will be able to proceed with an eviction action if the tenant persists in an unlawful denial of access to the property.

A landlord may enter the dwelling to inspect the premises, perform repairs, conduct standard maintenance, or show the premises to a prospective purchaser or renter. All of these are valid reasons for entry and will not subject the landlord to any potential penalties. It is when the landlord begins to abuse the right of entry, either through unnecessary or inconvenient visits, that a landlord may find him- or herself accused of unreasonably abusing the right of access.

When entering a tenant's unit in a nonemergency situation, provide notice of entry in writing. This is not to say that it is inappropriate to provide additional notice by telephone. However, it is not recommended that your only means of notice be by telephone. If it is, you do not have any documented proof of the notice in the event that your tenant accuses you of an unauthorized entry. If you provide notice in writing, a copy of that notice is your proof that you indeed provided legally sufficient notice of your entry into the dwelling.

Duty to Provide a Safe Environment

A landlord is not obligated to ensure a tenant's safety under all circumstances. Conversely, the landlord cannot ignore a tenant's safety, either. The landlord's duty falls somewhere in between. The landlord has a duty of *due care*, which includes reasonable steps to protect the safety of his or her tenants from foreseeable dangers, such as property damage or violent crime. *Foreseeable dangers* include those that the landlord could have anticipated in advance. If a landlord had no reasonable indication of the danger, then the danger was not foreseeable.

A landlord should take reasonable steps towards insuring the safety of his or her tenants. This includes taking reasonable steps to protect tenants against known or foreseeable criminal acts of their fellow tenants. If you have a reason to believe that a tenant is in danger from a possible criminal act committed by another resident, then you need to take some action. Some of the things you could do include taking appropriate action to control the other resident or warn the resident in danger of the potential problem. If you have no way of knowing the potential danger, then it is unlikely that the danger was foreseeable to the extent that you would become liable.

You also need to take reasonable steps to protect tenants from known dangerous conditions. For example, if you discover a large hole in the backyard, you should discuss the condition with the resident to ensure that the resident is aware of the condition. Random acts of violence are generally not going to be held against a landlord who has no reason to know of the threat. For example, a gunshot fired by an unknown third party down the street is not a foreseeable threat for which a landlord can be held responsible. Some general steps that a landlord can take to comply with the legal responsibilities in this area include the following.

◆ *Make certain that your basic security systems are in place and functioning correctly*. If you have security gates, community lock systems, or other means of preventing entry except to authorized residents, regularly check those systems for efficiency and accuracy.

◆ *Do not use claims in your advertising that will come back to haunt you.* No matter what level of security your properties provide, do not promise levels of security that are unattainable. It is impossible to guarantee that nothing will ever happen to your tenants as long as they live on your property. Therefore, do not promise that your properties are impenetrable.

◆ *Take care of your tenant's security needs as soon as is practical.* Make sure that you have a system of maintenance and repair ready to fix or replace any security items as soon as the need arises. Nothing will invite liability faster than ignoring or delaying a request from a tenant regarding a broken security device. Do not take that chance.

◆ *Check on the property at different times to ensure that it appears to be safe regardless of the time of day or night.*

◆ *Make sure that the exterior lighting systems are in place and functioning during all hours in which lighting is necessary.*

◆ *In larger urban areas with taller buildings, the expense of a twenty-four-hour doorman may be a worthwhile investment.*

◆ *The neighborhood of the property may dictate the level of security necessary.* If the property is adjacent to areas with bars or nightclubs, or in places where people tend to congregate late at night, the level of security will probably need to be higher than a property in a rural area. Consider the property in light of the nature of the area before settling on the appropriate level of security.

◆ *Do not invite criminal activity.* Landlords often unwittingly invite robbery by accepting large amounts of cash from tenants, sometimes late at night. Avoid cash if possible.

◆ *Screen your tenants carefully in the application process.* Run credit checks and ask about previous criminal convictions. Do not be afraid to probe prospective tenants about their criminal past. It will protect you, and potentially your residents, if you can obtain the requisite information. (Criminals are not a protected class under fair housing laws.)

◆ *Once you start having trouble with a resident, do not hesitate to send appropriate notices or begin eviction proceedings.* A landlord is inviting litigation by letting things go. It is important to deal with these situations promptly, even though it may have a negative impact on the occupancy. If you become aware of a tenant's propensity for violence, or have reason to believe that violence is possible, take immediate action to monitor or evict that tenant. Anything else may be an invitation to liability.

Property Managers

If you decide to hire a property manager or some other caretaker for your property, you will not automatically going to be liable for the criminal acts of that person. However, the landlord is not immune from liability, either. The landlord can be found liable for negligence in the hiring of people to take care of the property if it is found that the landlord did not investigate the person's background properly prior to hiring and probably should not have hired the person in the first place. It would be difficult to pin any liability on a landlord if there was no reason for a landlord to know prior to hiring that any criminal activity might occur (*i.e.*, no criminal history), and if the criminal activity occurs outside the scope of the manager's normal course of duties.

It is important to note that the greater access the hired person has to the tenants, the more responsibility the landlord has to check him or her out. A live-in property manager should definitely have his or her background checked, whereas the occasional snow removal person probably does not need the same check.

Insurance

If you own rental property, you should already know that insurance coverage is essential and that insurance needs to be of a sufficient amount. Insurance for a landlord can come in many forms. The following three types of coverage are the most important, and you should not be conducting business without them.

1. *Personal Liability covers injuries to tenants or innocent third parties on the premises.* Personal liability coverage is a must for any landlord. The type of personal injury can vary widely, ranging from a simple slip-and-fall incident to exposure to hazardous materials, housing discrimination, and all the way up to a wrongful death case. A landlord should never conduct business as if he or she is immune from a personal liability claim. These claims occur every day, and it is essential that you have an appropriate level of coverage for the amount of units that you own. Consult your insurance agent for more information if you have any reason to believe that your level of coverage may be insufficient.

2. *Property Insurance covers structural or physical damage to the dwelling not intentionally caused by the landlord.* Construction is not perfect. Residential property often sustains damage, even if the building is relatively young. Do not let the age of your property determine your property coverage. Consistently review your property coverage, particularly if you believe the value of your property is appreciating. You

always want to make sure that you have enough coverage to allow replacement of the property, if necessary.

3. *Loss of Rent Insurance covers rent lost in the event the property is uninhabitable for reasons not caused by the landlord, such as fire, flood, earthquakes, or even damage caused by a former tenant.* In these events, proper loss of rent coverage is essential, and your insurance agent should be able to walk you through the steps to realize the appropriate amount.

Limiting the Landlord's Duties

The parties can legally agree that the tenant will perform repairs or other services that would otherwise be the obligation of the landlord. In return, the tenant should receive some consideration or benefit from the landlord for performing these repairs or services. Typical forms of consideration include monetary payments or a reduction in the monthly rent. In order to be legal, the agreement between the parties to shift these responsibilities to the tenant must be based on a good-faith agreement between the parties and not as a means for the landlord to avoid a legal obligation.

The following are some general ideas to keep in mind if you and your tenant are considering shifting some of the maintenance or repair responsibilities to the tenant.

◆ Never entrust your tenant to make any major repair or maintenance tasks. There are several reasons for this. You may be inviting liability if the repairs lead to any personal injury. You may not be getting the level of expertise needed for the level of repair. Just because your tenant says he or she can fix it, does not mean he or she actually can. Lastly, the courts may find that the consideration provided to the tenant is inadequate if the repairs performed by the tenant are considered major.

◆ Any agreement with your tenant shifting the responsibility for repairs or maintenance should always be in writing. If your agreement is not in writing, your tenant may easily misrepresent the terms of the agreement and claim that you have not fulfilled your promises. (Having the agreement in writing may also help in avoiding the creations of an employer/employee relationship.)

◆ Keep the tenant's responsibilities confined to his or her own dwelling. If you start having the tenant perform services outside of his or her dwelling, it begins to look as if he or she is your employee. This could subject you to federal tax issues, such as Social Security withholdings, and make you personally liable for actions taken by the tenant.

Lastly, it is very important that you do not enter into any agreements with your tenants regarding repairs if hazardous materials (such as asbestos or lead-based paint) may be involved. In this event, do not mess around. Hire a licensed contractor or biohazard expert to perform any necessary services. State or federal law may require that a licensed contractor perform the repairs, depending on their nature.

Selling the Property

When you decide to sell a piece of property, you will undoubtedly want to ensure that there is no continuing liability after the completion of the sale. Take the following steps subsequent to the closing.

> **Landlord Tip**
>
> Providing notice to your tenants of an impending sale is an essential aspect of preventing any liability subsequent to the date of the sale. The notice should include the name and contact information for the new owner, along with the date that the property will officially change ownership.

◆ Notify each of the tenants of the date of the impending sale.

◆ Notify your tenants either by hand or by certified mail. This proof of delivery is essential for the landlord to rebut any contention that the tenant may pursue the landlord for any activity that occurs subsequent to the sale of the property.

◆ Make sure that your closing documents address your tenant's security deposit and how it will be transferred to the new owner. The rental agreement or lease remains in full force and effect, with the new owner assuming the rights and responsibilities of the previous owner.

Chapter 6:

Your Tenant's Rights, Remedies, and Duties

Virtually every state has enacted a series of laws designed to protect and further the rights of residential tenants. If you ignore the rights and remedies in the hands of your tenants, you can surely expect to find yourself defending a lawsuit. If a landlord violates the rental agreement through a material breach, a tenant has numerous rights (sometimes referred to as *remedies)*. The tenant may be able to terminate the lease, recover damages, or may be obligated to send a notice to the landlord as a prerequisite to further action. A material breach can be difficult to define, but it is generally a breach of sufficient influence or effect on the other party.

Some remedies require that a written notice be sent to the landlord and some do not. Remedies that do not require a notice are known as *self-help* remedies. In self-help cases, the tenant is permitted to make the necessary repairs and deduct the cost from his or her next rent payment.

The nature of the breach dictates whether a tenant's remedy may be achieved via a written notice or self-help. As a general rule of thumb, less serious breaches often warrant self-help remedies, while more serious breaches will warrant written notices. As tenant's rights have evolved in recent years, numerous rights and remedies have become available. It would be a colossal mistake to underestimate the rights and remedies available to your tenants.

When a Tenant can Employ a Remedy

A tenant may use a remedy any time the landlord is in *material breach*. A material breach is not something that either party can unilaterally define, but the following examples demonstrate instances of material breach.

◆ *If you fail to provide an essential service, such as water, heat, or electricity.* It does not matter where the premises is located or the amount of rent that you charge, you must provide these essential services to your tenants, regardless of the terms contained in your lease (even in the event you have no written lease).

◆ *If the tenant is wrongfully removed from the dwelling by either the landlord or a third party.* Once the landlord and tenant have entered into an agreement, that agreement is binding on both parties. The landlord has an obligation not to disturb the peaceful and quiet enjoyment of the premises during the course of the agreement. The landlord also has the obligation to prevent others under his or her control form disturbing that peace.

◆ *The tenant is prevented from moving into the dwelling by either the landlord or a third party.* A tenant will be able to recover damages, or possibly terminate the lease, if the dwelling to be rented is occupied by a third party. This is a prime example of the landlord's responsibility to regularly and thoroughly inspect his or her rental property, particularly just before a new tenant moves in.

◆ *The landlord does not give proper legal notice and makes an unlawful entry into the tenant's dwelling.* The landlord should always give a written notice before entering a tenant's dwelling. State statutes often specify the amount of advance notice required of a landlord (often between twenty-four and forty-eight hours). If the landlord enters a dwelling without proper notice, many state statutes allow for damages to be recovered from the landlord.

There are plenty of other circumstances in which a landlord may be in material breach, but these are examples that appear the most often.

Proper Notice of Material Breach from your Tenant

Tenants do have an obligation to give proper notice of a material breach. If the notice you receive is improper, or if you do not receive notice at all, a judge is likely to find that the improper notice acts as if no notice had ever actually been given in the first place. This puts the tenant back at square one but does not cure any problem. If the tenant is complaining about some repair, failing to take action on your part because of improper notice may make the repair that much more costly.

Only two methods ensure proper and legal delivery of the notice. The first is a notice delivered to the landlord by hand, after which the tenant could testify to the fact that the notice was actually received. Notice may also be sent to the landlord by certified mail, return receipt requested, with the landlord's signature providing proof that the notice was received.

You may try to avoid receiving notice by not signing for the certified mail. You probably will not be successful in this attempt. The courts are likely to find that a notice sent to a landlord by certified mail, return receipt requested, is an effective means of giving notice, and you will not be able to escape the notice merely by refusing to accept it. Thus, in this limited instance, you are likely to be bound by the notice—even if you never see it.

You can always agree to accept notice by any means you wish. The formal procedures are to satisfy the court if a dispute arises. However, if you establish a procedure that is more flexible (phone, fax, or email) than your state's statute, you will have to abide by it.

> **Landlord Tip**
>
> If one of your tenants does not strictly comply with the rules, do not assume that a court will absolutely strike the notice. State statutes regarding valid written notices are extremely clear, yet numerous judges simply give tenants *the benefit of the doubt.* In order to be safe, if a tenant complains about a problem that appears to be legitimate, and you can devise a solution, do so. You cannot rely on judges to always follow the strict letter of the law.

Accompanying Documentation

Any notice that you receive from a tenant concerning a material breach should include the nature of the breach, the dates and times that may be relevant, and an explanation of the time that the landlord has to fix the breach. Your tenant should be concise, but should include every important detail. Under your state law, you will have a certain number of days to address a material breach, and possibly fewer days to address a material breach involving health or safety. Along with the notice, an informed tenant may include pictures, video, health inspection reports, or any other evidence that supports the notice.

If your tenant does not necessarily comply with the procedures just referenced, it would be dangerous to assume that the notice is presumptively invalid. If your tenant reasonably identifies a necessary repair or maintenance item, take care of the problem in a timely fashion. Failure to do so only invites claims for damages and the right of your tenant to unilaterally terminate the lease.

Tenant's Action

If you ignore a notice of material breach, the tenant is far from helpless. After written notice has been delivered, the landlord has the opportunity to cure (fix) the alleged breach. If the landlord cures the breach within the appropriate time frame, the tenancy continues as before and the rental agreement is reinstated. If the landlord does not cure the breach within the appropriate time frame, the tenant has the legal right to terminate the tenancy and move out without any further liability to the landlord.

Self-Help Remedies

A tenant may use a *self-help remedy* when the unit is in need of some type of minor repair and the landlord has not taken corrective action. Remember, the right of self-help does not include costly repairs, such as a new roof or extensive renovations. The right only exists for minor defects, typically $300 or less. It is not available if the condition was caused by the tenant, the tenant's family, or a guest. If the tenant has followed the self-help procedures properly, including documentation of any work performed by a licensed contractor, the tenant may be able to deduct the actual and reasonable cost of the work from the next month's rent.

Problems between Cotenants

A tenant may find that he or she has issues with another resident. The rule to remember is that one tenant does not have the power to evict another tenant. (Only the landlord has the power to evict.) A responsible tenant will inform the landlord in writing of the problem, which gives the landlord the opportunity to act against the other tenant. If you become aware of a dispute between cotenants, remind them not to take the law into their own hands. However, remember that it is not advisable to try to intervene between warring tenants. You do not want to be perceived as choosing one tenant over another.

Home-Based Business

If your tenant indicates an intent to run a home-based business, regardless of the size, confirm that the property is properly zoned for business use. Before you approve the business, ask a lot of questions regarding the tenant's intended use. Even if you do consent to the use of the property for business purposes, confirm that your tenant will not conduct any business until all necessary permits and insurance policies are in place (particularly liability insurance).

Assigning the Lease

A lease is *assigned* when a new person steps into the shoes of the original tenant by assuming the rights of that tenant in the rental agreement and assuming possession of the premises. This may be a viable alternative when a tenant does not want to continue the tenancy, but is bound by the lease. Your tenant will generally need your permission in order to assign the lease to another party, and the other party will often have to go through the same steps that the original tenant did, including a rental application and credit check.

An assignment may be a viable alternative when the following are present.

- ◆ The present tenant cannot afford the rent and you are faced with an eviction action.
- ◆ The present tenant is not happy with the dwelling for some reason and offers a new resident, as opposed to you having to advertise or take other action to find a new tenant.
- ◆ The landlord is concerned about the tenant's ability to fulfill the terms of the lease and believes that an assignee of the lease may be a better alternative.

When the lease is assigned, remember that the new tenant is stepping into the shoes of the previous tenant. Absent an agreement for the original tenant to continue to be bound by the lease, the old tenant will be released from any future claims and the new tenant will be the only tenant you can look to for damages.

Take the following steps when assigning a lease.

- ◆ Treat the prospective new tenant (the assignee) as you would any new resident. Obtain a credit application and pursue your normal credit check procedures.

◆ Get the assignment in writing, and be sure it contains the consent of the old tenant (the assignor) and the new tenant, in addition to your signature.
◆ Make sure that the document assigning the lease from the old tenant to the new tenant includes any provisions that you may want, including keeping the original tenant liable for rent in the event that the new tenant is unable to pay.

The actual document assigning the lease does not have to be complicated, but should include:

◆ the names of the parties involved (landlord, assignor, assignee);
◆ the address of the dwelling;
◆ the date;
◆ the term of the original lease between the landlord and original tenant;
◆ the fact that the original tenant is giving up rights to the lease or rental agreement;
◆ the fact that the new tenant agrees to be bound by the terms and conditions of the original lease; and,
◆ the signatures of all three parties.

Subletting

Subletting refers to a situation whereby a third party assumes occupancy for a certain amount of time, with the understanding that the original tenant will eventually move back in. It may also involve an existing tenant renting out a part of the dwelling to his or her own subtenant while he or she remains in possession.

The original tenant remains liable for all of the lease terms. You have the right to approve or reject the occupancy of the subtenant. Subletting is often considered by tenants when they are planning to travel for an extended period of time or will be transferred to a new city for a certain amount of time, but will ultimately return.

It is also often considered in situations when a tenant wants to remain in possession of a dwelling, but is having a difficult time keeping up with the rent. In those cases, a subtenant acts as a roommate to the tenant, and can help him or her meet the rental obligations. However, a subtenant is not the same from your perspective as a situation in which multiple people rent one unit from you. If the subtenant's agreement is only with the tenant, you have a limited ability to go after the subtenant for damages. In a roommate situation, all parties sign the lease, so you have a direct agreement that you can enforce with each of the roommates.

It is important to remember what subletting is not. Implicit in the concept of subletting is that the new tenant assumes occupancy with the express consent of the landlord. If the landlord has not expressed consent, then the new occupant is not a sublessee, but rather an unauthorized occupant.

If your tenant gets married, the landlord is not bound to automatically accept the spouse as a tenant, but the original tenant is still bound by the terms of the lease. The parties may modify their agreement as they see fit to accommodate the new spouse, typically with the execution of a new agreement. However, the law will not hamstring the landlord into accepting a resident that the landlord would otherwise reject.

Subletting differs greatly from an assignment of the lease, although both usually require the landlord's approval. The are some specific characteristics of subletting. In a sublease, the landlord does not have a direct contractual relationship with the subtenant. In essence, the original tenant becomes the subtenant's landlord, and can deal with the subtenant as a landlord deals with an original tenant.

If a breach of the lease occurs that leads the landlord to an eviction action, the eviction will be against the original tenant, even if the breach is wholly caused by the subtenant. Remember, the landlord only has a contractual relationship with the original tenant, therefore, the landlord's eviction action will be against the original tenant. However, if the judge rules in favor of the landlord, both tenant and subtenant will be forced to move. If the tenant's rights to possess the dwelling are terminated, then it makes sense that any agreement between tenant and subtenant has implicity terminated.

Since subletting is different from an assignment, and the subtenant does not have a direct contractual relationship with you, you do not necessarily need the type of agreement required for an assignment. You will, however, want to make sure that subtenants meet with your approval and are acceptable under your lease or rental agreement, as they will be living in your property as a tenant. Appendix I has a sample landlord's form permitting a sublet.

Tenant's Guests

A tenant is not only responsible for his or her own actions, but will also be held responsible for the actions of his or her occupants and guests. If an occupant or guest commits a crime or breaches the lease in a material way, the tenant is the one that will be held responsible under the lease. An eviction action may proceed as if the violation was committed directly by the tenant. For this reason, do not hesitate to remind your tenants that they are responsible for occupants and guests. If your tenants think that one of their occupants or guests will violate the lease in any way, encourage them to think twice before allowing that person into their home.

Duties Regarding Roommates

For numerous reasons, people may choose to become roommates with others. While these roommates may believe that their responsibilities are separate, the landlord can take action against all roommates for a breach of the lease, even if only one roommate is responsible. This is known as *joint and several liability*.

If one roommate violates the lease, then everyone can be evicted. If one tenant does not pay his or her share of the rent, the landlord can look to the other roommates for the entire rent. The tenants can then fight amongst themselves to apportion their rightful shares and collect from one another. The important point to remember (as a practical matter) is that while you can only recover once, you can collect everything currently owed from any one roommate.

Roommates generally have no power to evict one another. A tenant can evict a subtenant, as the tenant and subtenant essentially have a landlord/tenant relationship, and the actual landlord has no direct relationship with the subtenant. Otherwise, it is the landlord with the power to evict—not the tenant.

In disputes amongst roommates, it is best to remain neutral with squabbling cotenants. You definitely do not want to be seen as taking sides, and should therefore steer as clear from these squabbles as possible. However, the roommates must understand that unless the landlord agrees to let them out of the lease, they are still bound by its provisions—even if they no longer live on the premises.

Chapter 7:

Terminating the Tenancy

Most tenancies do not end with an eviction action, but instead end because of other circumstances. This is often just the end of the tenancy, with the tenant moving to a new residence. However, there are procedures you should follow at the end of tenancy to make the transition as smooth as possible and to ensure that there will be as few problems as possible.

Move-Out Inspection

A wise landlord is not only concerned with the move-in inspection (see p.25), but pays particular attention to the move-out inspection as well. Prior to a tenant's moving out, a standard move-out letter is a good idea. This letter should:

- ◆ request that your tenant provide a forwarding address where the security deposit statement can be mailed;
- ◆ propose a date and time for a mutual move-out inspection of the dwelling; and,
- ◆ ask that the tenant perform basic cleaning or repairing as may be required, including the cleaning of carpets, painting, patching, or other minor items.

The move-out inspection will occur either as the tenant is moving out or immediately thereafter, and both parties should make themselves available. This is the opportunity for your tenant to convince you of any problems that should not lead to a security deposit deduction and for you to get a sense of the repair issues that you will encounter. At the inspection, you may agree to let the tenant perform some of the additional cleaning or other maintenance issues present, or you may want to reserve those for people you trust to handle those services.

At the move-out inspection, it is always a good idea to take lots of pictures or have a video camera to document the dwelling's condition. Pictures and videotape are an excellent way to document the condition of the dwelling before a tenant moves in and when he or she moves out. This is handy in the event that you pursue your tenant for damages or in the event that your tenant sues you, claiming that you have wrongfully withheld all or a part of the security deposit.

Once the move-out inspection is complete, even if the parties appear to have resolved any outstanding issues, keep your tenant's documentation, including the lease, tenant ledger, notices, and pictures and videotape of the dwelling, for several years. Many states allow suits based on contract to be brought years after the fact, so you want to be prepared in the event that your tenant sues you one, three, or five years later. (The amount of time that landlord and tenant may sue each other based on the tenancy is dictated by your state's statute of limitations on contract actions.) Memories may fade in the interim, but your pictures and documentation should help tell an accurate story.

Death of a Tenant

If a tenant living alone passes away during the course of a lease, the landlord is often left without any direction as to the status of the lease and the tenant's belongings. As an initial step, you should attempt to reach any emergency contacts for the tenant. If no emergency contacts are known, agencies such as the public fiduciary may become involved.

Even though your tenant has passed away, the lease does not automatically terminate. The estate of the deceased tenant is still responsible for the tenant's obligation, but the landlord is once again bound with a duty to mitigate damages by re-renting the premises as quickly as possible.

You should not allow the tenant's belongings to be removed without an appropriate probate court order authorizing the removal. Oral statements from a family member or attorney regarding those belongings are generally insufficient. If it appears that a probate court order might not come quickly, consider storing the deceased tenant's belongings, but take care to itemize those belongings.

There are several people who ultimately may be entitled to the tenant's belongings as long as they can produce evidence of that right in the form of a probate court order. These individuals include:

- ◆ the executor of the tenant's estate;
- ◆ a representative from the probate court (who is likely to become more involved if the decedent passed away without will); and,
- ◆ the heirs of the estate.

A decedent may pass away without the need for a formal probate proceeding. In that event, an heir may be entitled to remove property with a valid death certificate to go along with the tenant's will. If you have any reservations about the release of property, contact an attorney immediately. The rightful heirs of a decedent may have a claim against you if you release property inappropriately.

Since the passing of a tenant does not terminate the tenant's obligation under the lease, you may have to make a claim against a deceased tenant's estate. The deceased tenant's estate may be obligated to pay for:

- ◆ unpaid rent due at the time of the tenant's passing;
- ◆ unpaid rent during the balance of a lease prior to the unit being re-rented or the lease expiring under its own terms; and,
- ◆ costs of repairs or replacement for items in the dwelling.

If you believe that you need to make a claim against the estate of a former tenant, discuss the matter with an attorney before deciding how you will need to proceed. There are several factors that may dictate the appropriate course of action.

Active Duty Military Personnel

Active duty military personnel may be able terminate the lease without your consent. A federal law known as the *Soldiers' and Sailors' Civil Relief Act* provides that military personnel may be allowed out of their lease obligation if they are transferred to another location during the course of their tenancy. The active duty military member must be able to document transfer orders.

Fire or Casualty Damage

A lease may be terminated in the event of a fire or other event that substantially damages the dwelling or renders it uninhabitable. The key, however, is that the tenant cannot terminate the lease if the fire or other damage was caused by the tenant. As long as the tenant was not responsible, the tenant can argue that he or she is being constructively evicted as a result of the damage. *Constructive eviction* means that the dwelling is uninhabitable or unfit, and the tenant has no choice but to move.

In order for the tenant to terminate the lease based on this type of damage, the tenant will need to give a written notice to the landlord, specifying that the dwelling is uninhabitable and providing a date in which the tenant will be moving. The landlord will then have an opportunity to confirm the allegation of constructive eviction and contest the tenant's determination that the dwelling is uninhabitable.

Abandoned Property

Unfortunately for landlords, it is not that uncommon for tenants to simply abandon the premises without notice. When a tenant abandons the dwelling, personal property may be left behind. In this event, do not assume that you can simply throw the tenant's belongings out or take possession of the things you feel may have some value.

Many states have statutes providing for the disposition of abandoned personal property, and the landlord is required to follow the letter of the law. If a tenant wishes to retrieve property previously abandoned, he or she will need to contact you immediately, as you will not have the obligation to hold onto this personal property for a very long period of time. In Arizona, for example, this period is a short ten days after a tenant abandons a dwelling and twenty-one days after the completion of the eviction process. This period of time varies by state, so you should research your state's requirements.

Once the statutory period of time has passed, the landlord is able to discard any items believed to be of little or no value, or sell any items of value, with the proceeds applied to the tenant's outstanding balance. If you find yourself with a large amount of abandoned personal property, the first step should be to itemize the property. When that is complete, it is advisable to send a list of that property by certified mail to the tenant at the address of the dwelling.

Although the tenant is unlikely to receive the letter, this step allows you to show at a later date that reasonable attempts were made to inform the tenant of the disposition of the personal property. While you are holding the abandoned property, it may be kept in the dwelling, or you may decide to store it off-site, particularly if you hope to re-rent the dwelling quickly. If the tenant makes no effort to retrieve the property, many states allow you to dispose of the property if it is of no reasonable value or sell the property and apply the outstanding proceeds towards any balance owed by the tenant.

Retaliation

While a landlord has the right to terminate a tenancy for a variety of reasons, a termination cannot be *retaliatory*. A retaliatory eviction is one not based on any breach of the lease, but on a landlord's desire to throw out a tenant for doing something the landlord did not like. A tenant can argue that an eviction is retaliatory if one of the following circumstances is present.

- ◆ The tenant has filed a complaint concerning the state of the property with the landlord.
- ◆ The tenant has filed a complaint concerning the state of the property with a health or housing authority.
- ◆ The tenant is involved with some sort of tenant's union.

In order for an eviction to be retaliatory, the tenant must persuade the judge that the landlord does not have legitimate grounds to proceed with the eviction.

---**Landlord Tip**---

Not only is it a good idea for your tenants to carry renter's insurance, it would be prudent to recommend it as part of the lease. This insurance provides compensation for damages to the tenant's personal property as a result of theft, natural disaster, or the tenant's own negligence. The policy may also provide liability protection for personal injuries or property damage sustained by third parties.

---**Landlord Tip**---

A judge will likely find that evictions for nonpayment of rent are never retaliatory.

Chapter 8:

Evictions and Collection Actions

One of the hardest things for a new landlord to accept is that evictions are a necessary element of the business. Though never pleasant, evictions are an everyday occurrence for landlords across the country. A responsible landlord understands that a working knowledge of the legal system is absolutely vital. This chapter covers some of the basics you need to know, but does not provide a detailed discussion of the eviction court procedure.

An eviction may be for any variety of things, but all successful evictions share some common characteristics. These characteristics include:

- ◆ proper notice being delivered in proper fashion to your tenant;
- ◆ a demonstrated pattern of treating tenants in a consistent and even-handed manner; and,
- ◆ an understanding and compliance with your individual state statutes.

When in doubt about any of the steps to be taken or the procedures to follow in an eviction case, do not hesitate to contact knowledgeable legal counsel. The cost of an attorney pales in comparison to the penalties a landlord can face for violating the law.

Locking the Tenant Out or Turning Off Utilities

As long as the tenant is in compliance with the lease, a landlord cannot unilaterally lock out the tenant or turn off the utilities. Either of these actions will invite a lawsuit from the tenant for actual damages incurred, or for damages allowed under state statutes. Landlords sometimes forget that the lease is a two-way street, even though they own the property. Landlords are generally restricted from locking out tenants or turning off utilities until after an eviction has been completed and the tenant has been removed from the property, or after a landlord has completed the abandonment procedure. Only then do most state laws allow landlord to change the locks and shut off the utility connections.

The Need for an Attorney

Real property can be owned in a variety of ways beyond that of a single individual, such as in a partnership, trust, corporation, or one of many other assorted legal entities. If you are faced with an imminent eviction action, the form of ownership can make a big difference in your ability to proceed without an attorney.

Single individual owners can represent themselves without an attorney. Multiple owners who are involved in a partnership, trust, corporation, or other legal entity are often unable to proceed without an attorney.

> **Landlord Tip**
>
> A corporation is considered a legal person separate from its owners. So even if you own all the stock of a corporation and are its only employee, it is still a separate person from you in the eyes of the law.

The law allows a person to represent him- or herself in court. However, if you have formed a partnership with someone else or incorporated your business, you need an attorney to represent that business. There may be exceptions to this, such as if an individual has a corporate authorization allowing his or her to proceed in an eviction action. However, do not count on exceptions, and understand that you may have no choice but to use an attorney if the property is owned by any entity other than a sole individual.

While the necessity of hiring an attorney is a decision facing landlords every day, the answer always depends on the circumstances involved. Hiring an attorney is a good idea if you encounter any of the following.

- Any time there is a current or looming dispute with a tenant.
- Your tenant has just filed a bankruptcy petition.
- You are an out-of-town landlord and it is inconvenient to handle the eviction process on your own.
- You are considering an eviction action and your tenant lives in an area governed by rent control.

The recovery of attorney's fees in the event of a court action may be easier than you think. If your lease or rental agreement provides that the prevailing party in any court action is entitled to the recovery of his or her attorney's fees, the courts usually follow this provision and award them.

Attorneys can be beneficial for landlords in a variety of ways, including:

◆ writing or reviewing leases or rental agreements between the landlord and tenant, including subsequent modifications;

◆ discussing everyday issues with you involving notices that may be appropriate for your tenant or discussing the legality of any action desired by the landlord;

◆ representing landlords in eviction or collection actions, or actions in front of any judicial or administrative body regarding a complaint made by a tenant; and,

◆ advising landlords as to whether any action or notice is against the law or a fair housing regulation.

Finding the Right Attorney for You

The right attorney for you depends on a number of factors. For many, a key factor is the price charged by the attorney. This price may be determined by the hourly rate he or she charges, on a per eviction basis, or in limited circumstances, through a contingency agreement. A *contingency agreement* means that the attorney is entitled to a portion of any money recovered from a tenant. This percentage is often ⅓ of the amount collected. Hourly rates throughout the country will vary widely, but it would be reasonable to assume that the average rate will be between $125 and $250 an hour.

If you and your attorney agree on representation by the hour, keep this in mind—your monthly bills will be much lower if you follow some simple rules when calling or meeting with your attorney. Have your questions ready in advance and write them down if necessary. You may also save money by doing some of the research on your own. Virtually every state has its landlord/tenant statutes on the Internet. Do not be afraid to conduct some research on your own, as it can save you a significant amount of unnecessary attorney's fees.

An attorney may or may not request a retainer from you (as well as a retainer agreement, which spells out the terms and conditions of the representation). A retainer ensures that the attorney will receive some compensation up front for contemplated services. Be careful, though, as an attorney does not necessarily need a large retainer from most landlord clients. If an attorney asks for more than $1,000 in advance (except in the event that complex litigation appeared imminent), be skeptical of that attorney's fee practice.

The knowledge and experience level of the attorney you hire is another factor. Attorneys are not versed in all areas of the law. Some are experts in criminal law, some are experts in family law, and others may be experts in wills and trusts. Relatively few attorneys are well-versed in landlord/tenant law. Just because an attorney may claim to have some experience in the area, do not be afraid to ask questions regarding his or her specific experience in court and whether the attorney also represents tenants. An attorney who also represents tenants may not be the strong advocate you need.

The availability of the attorney should also be considered. Few things annoy customers more than a failure to return calls. Landlord/tenant matters often require quick action and you need an attorney that is appropriately responsive to your needs. If your attorney cannot return your call for a few days, it is probably time to find a new attorney.

Material and Irreparable Breach

Sometimes a violation occurs that cannot be cured by the tenant since the violation itself is of a serious or criminal nature. When a breach of this nature occurs, many states allow for a landlord to proceed with immediate eviction. Examples of material and irreparable breach include the following.

◆ *Engaging in serious property damage.* Minor property damage is unlikely to suffice.
◆ *Prostitution on the premises.* In order to prevail in court, the landlord will need witnesses or evidence of arrest. Mere hearsay or rumors will not suffice.

♦ *Gang activity.* Similar to a charge of prostitution, the landlord needs witnesses or evidence of arrest.

♦ *Illegal discharge of a weapon.*

♦ *The unlawful manufacturing, sale, or possession of drugs.*

♦ *Homicide.*

♦ *Assault.*

♦ *Threatening or intimidating another resident or the property manager.* This charge requires the testimony of the resident or property manager threatened, but often these people are afraid to testify. Unfortunately, their testimony is crucial in these cases, and a landlord may not be able to proceed without it.

If a material breach occurs on the premises and is attributed to the tenant or the tenant's guests, the law generally states that the violation cannot be cured under any circumstances. This is even true in the event that the tenant had nothing at all to do with the violation. If a material and irreparable breach occurs on the premises and the tenant is the reason for the perpetrator to have been there, then the tenant is likely to be evicted. In fact, the tenant may be subject to immediate eviction, provided that a written notice terminating the tenancy is properly delivered.

Written Notices

For the landlord, the preparation and delivery of notices is a vital task, yet many do not understand the basics of delivering a valid notice. If you take one thing away from this book, it should be that oral notices will probably not be valid. The reasoning for this makes sense as is much more difficult to prove in a court of law that a notice was delivered if it was delivered orally.

Notices of any nature should always be in writing, and should include the tenant's name and address, the date, and the specifics of the notice, including the time that the tenant may have to cure the violation. If the notice is for nonpayment, the time frame for payment should be specified. For noncompliance, the nature of the violation should be specified, along with the time allowed to cure.

───── **Landlord Tip** ─────

You may ask, *What if I cannot catch the tenant personally to deliver the notice, and he or she does not pick up the certified letter?*

Under the URLTA, the tenant (and landlord, for that matter) are deemed to have received notice on the day it is actually received, or five days after the notice is mailed, whichever occurs first. In non-URLTA states, you will need to research your own state law or consult an attorney on this question.

Once a written notice contains proper specifics, the notice must be delivered properly to your tenant. Hand delivery of a notice is always appropriate, and the notice should contain a space for the tenant's signature, acknowledging delivery. Certified mail, return receipt requested, is also appropriate, and should be the other method of delivery considered. Sending the notice by first class mail is not a suggested method of delivery. Taping the notice to the front door may be allowed in your state under limited circumstances, but is generally not a good idea. These methods provide no proof of delivery admissible in court in the event that your tenant claims never to have received the notice.

Material Noncompliance

Before initiating an eviction action, you must decide if the tenant is actually in violation of the rental agreement. If the rent has not been paid, the decision is fairly easy, but if the rental agreement calls for a material noncompliance with its terms, the decision can become a little more complicated.

Material noncompliance refers to a breach by a tenant that is sufficiently serious to warrant you to put the tenant on notice that an eviction suit could be initiated. The problem, however, is that under most states laws, a breach of a rental agreement creates a correctable problem that the tenant must be notified of and given the chance to cure. It is not until after the period of time available for the cure has passed that the eviction procedures may begin.

Examples of material noncompliance that, if left uncorrected, can lead to an eviction include the following.

- ◆ *Unauthorized occupants living in the property.* The lease or rental agreement specifies the names of all parties allowed to reside in the dwelling. While a tenant is allowed to have guests, the landlord has a right to restrict these third parties if they have moved from guests to occupants. A good rule of thumb is that an *occupant* is a person residing at the dwelling more than fourteen days in a calendar month.
- ◆ *Unauthorized pets.* Your tenants are limited to the pets allowed under your lease or rental agreement. If your tenant's pets have babies, you are not necessarily required to allow those babies.
- ◆ *Disturbing the peaceful and quiet enjoyment of other residents (usually excessive noise).* This is always a subjective matter, as no objective criteria are available to tell how much noise is too much. The threshold

tends to involve complaints from the neighbors and the frequency of these complaints.

♦ *Junked cars in the driveway.* Vehicles that are currently inoperable and do not appear to be made operable anytime soon can be both an eyesore and a magnet of danger for potential injuries.

♦ *Failure to maintain the property.* This is a type of noncompliance that often results in evictions. A tenant's failure to maintain the property can result in a reduction in the property value and can force a landlord to incur considerable expense to restore the property to the condition at the beginning of the lease.

This is one of the reasons that it is incumbent for a landlord or property manager to physically inspect rental property on a regular basis. Once a tenant receives a written noncompliance notice, one of three things can happen. If the tenant corrects the violation within the time frame contained in the notice, the rental agreement is reinstated and the parties continue as they were. If the tenant does not correct the violation, you have two distinct options—file for eviction as soon as the period contained in the notice has expired or wait and see if the tenant violates the lease in a similar fashion at a later date.

Many states, including those governed by the URLTA, provide that a landlord has the right to terminate a tenancy upon a second notice for material noncompliance for the same or a similar infraction during the remainder of the time that the tenant resides at the dwelling. This option is often attractive for landlords if they believe that no further breaches of the lease will occur subsequent to the time frame referenced in the first notice.

> **Landlord Tip**
>
> Under your state statutes, a tenant may not have the right to repeatedly cure a recurring violation. The URLTA specifies that a landlord has the right to terminate a tenancy if an additional act of noncompliance of the same or similar nature occurs during the remainder of a tenancy.

Under this line of reasoning, if no further breaches occur, then the landlord continues to have a financially rewarding tenancy and does not need to incur the trouble and expense of an eviction. However, if the tenant does violate the lease in a similar way at a later date, the URLTA provides that the tenant does not have the right to cure these subsequent violations, and the landlord can file for eviction once the notice period passes—whether the tenant has cured or not. This puts the landlord in a position of relative strength.

Notices for Material Noncompliance

A landlord may pursue a remedy any time a tenant is in material breach of the contract. As stated in Chapter 6, a material breach is generally considered to be a breach of sufficient influence or effect on the other party. The landlord can only take action when a tenant is in material breach of the agreement. If it is a breach that the law considers insignificant, the landlord does not have a remedy available.

When faced with a material breach, the landlord has several options, depending on the nature of the breach. Those options include the following.

◆ *Warn the tenant that you will not tolerate further instances of material breach.* This warning can be verbal or written, but it is always advisable to document everything in writing. This helps in the event that you need to proceed with further action at a later date.

◆ *Providing the tenant with a written notice documenting the nature of the breach and how the breach may be corrected.* The written notices should be detailed, including the date, the nature of the breach, and the time allowed for the tenant to cure (fix) the breach.

◆ *Proceeding with an eviction action after an appropriate notice has been provided to the tenant.* An eviction action means that the landlord is considering the lease or rental agreement terminated and will be seeking possession of the dwelling.

◆ *Deciding not to renew a tenant's lease at the expiration of the lease or sending appropriate notice that a month-to-month tenancy will be terminated.* Depending on the nature of the breach and the length of time left in the tenancy, you may decide to accept certain behavior until the lease expires or until a month-to-month agreement has been terminated in hopes that the tenant will move out and avoid having to use the eviction procedure.

Forcible Entry and Detainer (Eviction) Actions

A *forcible entry and detainer*, also known as an *unlawful detainer*, is nothing more than a fancy term for *eviction*. The legal purpose of a forcible entry and detainer action is primarily to recover possession of the premises from the tenant, although the award of money damages is often a primary issue for the landlord. These proceedings are generally speedy, with the parties appearing in court much faster than they would in a typical civil lawsuit.

Landlords should be filing these actions after a written notice. These eviction actions are typically based on:

- ◆ nonpayment of rent;
- ◆ a material breach of the rental agreement unrelated to health and safety, such as unauthorized occupants or disturbing the peaceful and quiet enjoyment of neighbors;
- ◆ a material breach of the rental agreement related to health and safety, such as a dangerous condition on the property; or,
- ◆ a material breach of a sufficient nature to warrant an immediate eviction, such as an assault or other type of physical violence, prostitution, or drug possession or distribution.

The Complaint

The proceedings are initiated by the landlord filing a *Complaint*. This legal document sets out the names of the parties, the landlord's claim, and the landlord's request for relief from the court. An eviction complaint is typically a rather simple document, and your local courts may even supply a preprinted form for your convenience.

In an eviction action, the landlord is the Plaintiff and the tenant is the Defendant. Once the landlord files the Complaint, that Complaint must be served on the tenant. This means that the tenant must be notified of the eviction by a neutral third party in the business of delivering legal paperwork. These *process servers* are generally sheriff's deputies or others licensed by the state and are required to submit an affidavit of service to the court describing the method of serving the paperwork on the tenant.

Acceptable methods of serving paperwork include:

- ◆ serving the tenant in person;
- ◆ serving a person at the tenant's dwelling that is of suitable age and discretion (generally teenagers or older); or,
- ◆ if the tenant is unavailable, and no one can be found at the dwelling, the landlord may be authorized under state law to have the process server post the paperwork on the front door, and then send the paperwork to the tenant by certified mail.

Please be mindful, none of the options referenced above include the landlord delivering the paperwork personally. Professional process servers should always be employed. (The actual court proceedings involved in an eviction are beyond the scope of this book.)

Bankruptcy Considerations

There are few things more frightening to a landlord than receiving a notice that a tenant has filed a bankruptcy petition. While a bankruptcy petition can cause some undue stress, the landlord is equipped with some remedies in this event.

Once a bankruptcy petition is filed, a trustee will be appointed. This person will eventually evaluate the case and determine whether the bankruptcy debtor is entitled to a discharge, whether a Chapter 13 repayment plan is appropriate, or whether the bankruptcy petition should not have been filed in the first place.

The filing of a bankruptcy petition automatically halts (or *stays)* any current legal action against the tenant. Do not take this lightly. If you receive notice of a bankruptcy filing, you cannot proceed with any imminent or pending court actions against the tenant. In this event, contact an attorney immediately to discuss the type of petition that was filed, your rights to collect rent and other fees due both before and after the petition was filed, and the effects of the bankruptcy petition on your lease.

If a tenant is not in compliance with the lease after a petition has been filed, and the tenant reaffirms the lease, the landlord may go to the bankruptcy court and file a motion to lift the automatic stay. This is the landlord's request to pursue the tenant in state court for an alleged breach of the lease. The landlord is successful if the judge lifts the stay and allows the landlord to proceed with a case in the appropriate state court.

Post-Tenancy Lawsuits and Collection Actions

One of the most frustrating aspects of the eviction process is the attempt to recover money due from a former tenant. Regardless of whether a tenancy was terminated through eviction or the natural expiration of the rental agreement, the landlord retains the right to pursue a tenant for any damages incurred in excess of the tenant's security deposit. These damages may include necessary repairs that are beyond reasonable wear and tear or it may include a request for rent not awarded during an eviction.

If you have evicted your tenant, it is likely that you received a money judgment at that time, but you may have suffered additional damages after retaking possession from the tenant. You may not have a money judgment at all if the tenancy naturally expired. If you pursue a tenant for damages, you are looking for the court to award you a *judgment*, which is a court order specifying how much is legally owed by the tenant to the landlord. These judgments are interest-bearing, with the amount of interest determined on a state-by-state basis (generally, 10%).

Until you have a money judgment in hand, your claim is not legally binding on anyone. Once a money judgment is obtained, you have the legal right to collect the money provided in that judgment to the fullest extent of the law.

One of the most important keys to collecting from a former tenant involves the original credit application. Did you obtain valid employment information? Contact information? A Social Security number? Banking information? Obtaining valuable information before the tenancy can help a landlord collect money due from the tenant once the judgment is obtained.

If the original credit application includes employment information, call the tenant's employer to confirm that your former tenant is still employed. If so, you can institute an *earnings garnishment* against the wages of your former tenant. The court will issue the garnishment action, and the paperwork will need to be delivered to the employer.

The employer will then have the chance to file an *Answer*, stating whether or not the person is still employed. If the person is still employed, the employer will need to provide information regarding the amount of his or her wages. By law, you will only be able to garnish a certain amount of your former tenant's paycheck.

If the employer confirms the employment, and monies are available for garnishment, you then need the judge to sign an order directing the employer to withhold appropriate funds for payment on the judgment, with those funds being sent to the landlord. (The landlord, in this instance, is referred to as the *judgment creditor*.) Monies should continue to be garnished until the judgment is paid in full or the employment of your former tenant is terminated.

If you do not have employment information, review the credit application carefully for banking information. Bank accounts can be garnished as well, subject to your individual state's exemptions. States will often set a minimum amount in a bank account that is exempt from garnishment. If possible, it is advisable to have information about the balance in an account prior to garnishment.

In reality, this information is often very difficult to obtain and seems to be only getting more difficult. What you can normally obtain is information about whether the account is still active. If it is, it is often worth the risk of finding no available money to proceed with the bank garnishment. Even if no funds are available, it may shake up your former tenant enough to come to the table and try to resolve the debt.

If all you have is a Social Security number, you might consider hiring an asset locating firm. These firms are located around the country and can generally conduct asset or employment searches for a fixed price. If nothing else, these firms may be able to locate a current address for your former tenant, which is beneficial to your collection efforts.

Recording Your Judgment

In addition to any other post-judgment collection efforts, you should record the judgment in the county in which your former tenant resides. The recording process puts the world on notice of your former tenant's debt and serves as a lien on any real property owned by your former tenant. While this may not bear fruit in the short term, older judgments will often be paid off when someone attempts to buy, sell, or refinance a piece of real property many years down the road.

In order to properly record your judgment, contact your local county recorder's office. Your county recorder will probably require that your judgment be certified by the court before it can be recorded. While the amounts may be minimal, you will probably incur a fee in having your judgment certified, as well as a fee from the recorder's office to actually record the judgment.

> **Landlord Tip**
>
> It is important to remember the landlord's duty to mitigate damages if a tenant vacates before the end of the lease. The landlord cannot simply sit on his or her hands until the end of a lease and expect the tenant to be held responsible. The landlord always needs to be mindful of the duty to make a reasonable attempt to re-rent a dwelling as soon as is practical.

Chapter 9:

Accounting and Tax Considerations

As with any other venture for profit, rental property demands that you maintain good records in addition to your tenant files. Your financial records should be organized in a clear and logical manner, as haphazard records are an invitation for disaster (as well as an IRS audit). In addition to maintaining accurate checkbooks, accounting software is available that can help maintain computerized books for each of your properties if the need arises. The intent of the following material is to give you an overview of some of the issues encountered by landlords, but only a CPA or tax attorney is truly qualified to give you reliable tax advice.

Schedule E

The rental activities of an individual taxpayer are reported on page one of Schedule E, for IRS Form 1040. If an individual owns multiple rental properties, each property's income and expenses should be listed separately. Therefore, it is advisable to maintain separate checking accounts for each individual property. There may be instances in which expenses for one property are paid out of the landlord's personal account or from the account of a separate property. In that event, a check should be written out of the account for the property incurring the expense to reimburse the account of the property that initially paid the expense.

Passive Income and Losses

A *passive activity* is an investment in a trade or business without material participation. This will probably include your rental properties. There are exceptions to this rule, but rental income is generally considered passive.

Other types of passive activities include royalties earned from oil, gas, or mineral rights, copyrights or patents, or estate and trust income. Passive gains or losses are combined on IRS Form 8582 and are used in figuring an individual's Form 1040.

When passive gains are reported for the year, the income is taxed at normal rates but is not subject to *self-employment tax*. If a property results in a passive loss, the deduction is generally limited to the extent of the passive gain for the same period. Excess passive losses may be carried over to the next tax year.

Capital Gains Taxes

Capital gains taxes refer to the taxes owed on profits from the sale of capital assets. Rental property would obviously fall into the category of a capital asset. A short-term capital gain (or loss) involves assets held for one year or less, while long-term capital gains or losses refer to assets held for more than a year.

If you happen to have both short- and long-term capital transactions within the same year, each transaction will be reported separately, and the net short- and long-term capital gains or losses will be combined to arrive at an overall gain or loss for the year.

The capital gains tax rate is generally lower than the income tax rate and in most instances will be 15%. A CPA can provide more information on specific capital gains rates for your situation.

1031 Exchanges

A popular method of avoiding capital gains tax rates involves a transaction known as a *1031 Exchange*. These types of exchanges are advantageous for property that will subject the owner to a net gain upon sale. Rental property will ordinarily qualify.

The rules for a 1031 Exchange are fairly simple and straightforward. The property sold and the property bought must be *like-kind*, such as investment property for investment property. The proceeds from the sale go to a *qualified intermediary* (such as an attorney or title company experienced in these types of exchanges) before being used for the purchase of the new property. All of the proceeds from the sale must go into the *replacement property*. Any proceeds not put into the new property will be considered taxable.

In order to qualify, the seller of the original property must identify a suitable replacement property within forty-five days of the sale. The transaction on the replacement property must close within 180 days after the closing date on the sale of the original property. These deadlines are strict, so you should always maintain close contact with your intermediary to confirm that you are staying within the boundaries of the rules.

Sole Ownership and Entity Formation

Historically, the primary method of owning real property for a single individual has been as a *sole owner*. This means that the individual owns the property in his or her own name, and profits are taxed to the property owner—even if the owner does not take money out of the business. The obvious problem for sole owners is the potentially unlimited amount of liability they face. For this reason, both individual and jointly-held property owners have increasingly turned to business entities to shield themselves from liability to the greatest extent possible.

If a sole owner is looking for a measure of protection, they may look to the formation of a sole-member *limited liability company* (LLC). An LLC is registered with the state and typically involves the filing of some type of articles. An LLC is taxed like a partnership but can provide some liability protection like a corporation. Personal liability may still occur if a personal guarantee is required by any creditor, but if no personal guarantee is required, the individual may be able to avoid personal responsibility. If you desire further information on the benefits and obligations of various types of entities, do not hesitate to contact a local CPA or tax attorney.

If two or more partners are involved in the ownership, they may have a *general partnership* in which the partners share ownership, profits, losses, and liability—and no formal entity is required to register with the state. In a general partnership, the partners can split profits or losses any way they choose, and the partners address items such as profit and loss allocation, payments, and dispute resolution through the use of an operating agreement.

The central problem with a general partnership is the liability of each partner for the acts of the other partner. For this reason, many partners decide to form legal entities, and for different tax or liability reasons, may choose one of the following entities:

- ◆ a limited partnership;
- ◆ a limited liability company; or,
- ◆ a limited liability partnership.

The differences between these types of entities is admittedly subtle, and any consideration of any of these entities should include your local CPA or tax attorney.

Business Deductions

One, and perhaps the best, advantage of owning your own rental property is the tax advantage allowing you to take legitimate business deductions. *Legitimate* needs to be stressed, as owners have been known to push the envelope from time to time.

The following is a list of deductions that are perfectly reasonable for your rental property. Consult your local CPA or tax attorney as to other items that you would like to deduct but may not appear on this list.

- ◆ Payroll
- ◆ Bonuses
- ◆ Sick pay
- ◆ Vacation pay
- ◆ Health-care coverage
- ◆ Other employee expenses

These deductions should remain in play whether you employ actual employees of your business or use workers as independent contractors:

- ◆ various types of insurance on your property, including liability coverage, fire, and flood insurance;
- ◆ fees that you pay to professionals, such as attorneys or CPAs, for work done in relation to the property during the course of the year;
- ◆ property taxes;

◆ interest on mortgages or notes secured by your property;

◆ automobile expenses, including the choice between a standard deduction for the miles driven relating to the property or actual expenses incurred for your vehicle during the tax year; and,

◆ other miscellaneous deductions for things like licenses, advertising, or educational expenses.

Landlord Checklist

☐ Provide your tenant with a copy of the complete rental agreement and all addendums.

☐ Make sure that all blank spaces in your lease have been properly filled out.

☐ Keep copies of all receipts for rent or other charges paid.

☐ Inspect the premises before you sign the lease.

☐ Make sure that any notices received for repairs or other reasons are in writing.

☐ Make yourself available for the move-out inspection.

☐ Make sure you receive all keys at the time your tenants move out.

☐ Obtain forwarding addresses when your tenants move out.

☐ Do not accept cash. Stick to checks, money orders, or cashier's checks.

☐ Treat all of your tenants consistently.

☐ Properly document your reasons for rejecting any applicant.

☐ Make sure that all prospective tenants have fully filled out their rental application.

☐ Make sure that all of your notices are in writing and always keep copies of every notice given to your tenants.

☐ Do not accept partial payments without a signed partial payment agreement.

☐ Do not be afraid to inspect your rental property regularly—you own it!

☐ Keep tenant files up-to-date, accurate, and thorough.

☐ Make sure that you have a responsible maintenance person and that your tenants can reach the person.

Glossary

A

abandoned property. Personal property of the tenant left behind after the tenant vacates the dwelling.

actual damages. The actual monetary damage that a landlord can prove has been caused by a tenant's breach of the lease.

addendum. A mutual agreement by the parties to add a provision to the lease, executed at the same time the lease is executed.

agreement for a term. A written lease that specifically states the length of the tenancy.

assignment of the lease. Occurs when a new tenant steps into the shoes of the existing tenant by assuming possession of the premises and assuming the rights of the tenant under the original lease.

B

bankruptcy discharge. When a bankruptcy court allows a person to wipe out his or her debts.

boilerplate language. The basic terms and conditions that will generally be found in any standard rental agreement.

C

classes. Categories of people protected from discrimination.

commercial real property. Real property that is used for business or industrial purposes.

complaint. The document filed by a plaintiff in a court case, setting out the names of the parties, the claim, and a request for relief from the court.

constructive eviction. Claimed by the tenant when a dwelling becomes uninhabitable or unfit, and he or she reasonably has no choice but to move.

cosigner. A person who signs the lease along with the tenant but does not actually reside in the dwelling. Cosigners are generally required when the landlord is worried about the tenant's ability to fulfill the financial terms of the lease.

D

Department of Housing and Urban Development (HUD). A government agency that promotes fair housing principles and can provide certain types of relief for aggrieved parties.

disclosures. The blank spaces in the rental agreement that require individual information, including certain information that may be required by state law.

drop boxes. A place designated by the landlord in which tenants can deposit their rent at any hour of the day or night.

duty to deliver possession to tenant. Once a rental agreement has been executed by landlord and tenant, the landlord has an obligation to allow the tenant to actually move into the dwelling. The landlord can be held responsible if the tenant is denied occupancy, even if it is not necessarily as a result of any action by the landlord.

duty to maintain fit premises. The landlord typically has an ongoing obligation to keep essential services, such as water and electricity, in good working order.

duty to mitigate damages. In the context of landlords and tenants, a landlord has a duty to mitigate its damages. This means that the landlord must make reasonable efforts to minimize damages incurred as a result of a breach by the tenant.

dwelling. A home, apartment, mobile home, or other structure used as a sleeping place for one or more residents.

E

essential services. These include those services that are necessary to keep a dwelling habitable, such as water, heat, and electricity.

F

Fair Housing Amendments Act of 1988. Expanded on the *Federal Civil Rights Act of 1968* by prohibiting discrimination against the handicapped and families with children.

Federal Civil Rights Act of 1968. Prohibits discrimination on the basis of race, color, religion, sex, national origin, or age.

fire and casualty damage. Damage caused by fire, flood, or other natural disasters that renders a dwelling uninhabitable. These do not include damages caused by the tenants themselves.

foreseeable dangers. Danger of injury that could reasonably have been seen. The law expects the landlord to take reasonable steps to protect the safety of their tenants.

H

hazardous conditions. Within the scope of residential housing, lead-based paint and asbestos are two of the hazardous conditions for which to watch. Tenants should contact the landlord immediately if there is any sign of danger from these hazardous conditions.

I

implied provisions. Certain provisions will be implied to the lease, even though they are not specifically written. Examples include the warranty of habitability, which requires a landlord to provide a minimum level of habitability for the tenant.

J

joint and several liability. A legal principle, which holds that tenants may be both individually and collectively liable for any amounts owed to the landlord.

L

landlord. The party that rents a dwelling to a tenant.

lease. The contract that binds landlords and tenants together through a series of terms and conditions.

liquidated damages. A clause in the rental agreement that provides that the tenant will pay a certain amount to the landlord for a specified breach of the lease.

M

material breach. A breach of the lease by either landlord or tenant that has a sufficient influence or effect on the other party.

material irreparable breach. A breach of the lease that is not only material, but also cannot be corrected. (Examples include assault and drug possession.)

modifications. A mutual agreement by the parties, during the course of the lease, to modify a term or condition of the lease. The modification remains in effect for the remainder of the lease term.

move-in inspection. This is the opportunity for both landlord and tenant to document the condition of the dwelling at the time that the tenant is moving in, and the opportunity for the landlord to address any items that need repair at that time.

move-out inspection. This is the opportunity for both landlord and tenant to document the condition of the dwelling at the time that the tenant moves out. This inspection should be used in conjunction with the move-in inspection to determine appropriate tenant responsibility for items that need repair or replacement after the tenant has left.

N

nonrefundable deposits. The part of the security deposit that will not be returned to the tenant at the end of the lease. These nonrefundable deposits are usually earmarked for the cleaning or redecorating of the dwelling.

notice of nonpayment of rent. A written notice from the landlord to the tenant specifying any and all amounts due, and providing the time allowed by state law to pay those amounts.

O

oral rental agreement. Less preferable than a written rental agreement, an oral rental agreement contains the essential terms of a tenancy without a written document.

P

partial payment agreements. An agreement between the parties that the tenant will pay a portion of the amounts due on specific date(s), with a certain date when the final payment is due.

prohibited provisions. Certain provisions of a contract may be prohibited by state or federal law, and neither party can legally waive certain rights or remedies that they would otherwise have.

R

reasonable wear and tear. Generally considered to be the wear and tear that would be expected on a dwelling based on the age and condition of the dwelling, coupled with the length of the tenancy.

refundable deposits. The part of the security deposit that the tenant may be entitled to receive at the end of the lease, depending on the condition of the dwelling at that time.

remedies. Refers to the potential avenues that landlords and tenants if the other party has breached the rental agreement.

rent control. A system for limiting the rent increases that a landlord can impose on the tenant.

rental agreement. *See lease.*

residential real property. A house, apartment, condominium, mobile home, or any type of home where a tenant resides.

S

security deposit. A certain amount of money deposited by the tenant prior to commencement of the lease to assure the landlord of the tenant's full and faithful performance.

security deposit statement. A written statement provided by the landlord after the end of the tenancy. It itemizes the amount of the tenant's deposits followed by an accounting of the deductions from the deposits.

self-help remedies. These are the remedies that a tenant may use when the dwelling is in need of some type of repair and the landlord has yet to correct the problem.

Soldiers' and Sailors' Civil Relief Act. A federal law that allows certain military members out of their lease obligation if they are transferred to another location during the course of their tenancy.

statute of frauds. A legal precedent that dictates that leases of more than one year must be in writing in order to be enforceable.

subletting. Subletting occurs when a tenant allows a third party to assume occupancy of the dwelling during all or part of the rental agreement between the landlord and the tenant.

T

tenant. The party that rents a dwelling from a landlord.

U

Uniform Residential Landlord and Tenant Act (URLTA). The Act laid the basic framework for many of our current landlord and tenant laws. Its provisions have been adopted by a large number of states.

W

warranty of habitability. The warranty of habitability requires that the landlord keep up the premises to a minimum level of habitability, regardless of the rental agreement.

writ of restitution. The writ entitles the landlord to use a law enforcement officer to remove the tenant from the premises if the tenant does not leave voluntarily.

wrongfully withheld deposits. These are funds that are kept by the landlord without cause.

Appendix A:

Landlord Checklist

- ☐ Provide your tenant with a copy of the complete rental agreement and all addendums.
- ☐ Make sure that all blank spaces in your lease have been properly filled out.
- ☐ Keep copies of all receipts for rent or other charges paid.
- ☐ Inspect the premises before you sign the lease.
- ☐ Make sure that any notices received for repairs or other reasons are in writing.
- ☐ Make yourself available for the move-out inspection.
- ☐ Make sure you receive all keys at the time your tenants move out.
- ☐ Obtain forwarding addresses when your tenants move out.
- ☐ Do not accept cash. Stick to checks, money orders, or cashier's checks.
- ☐ Treat all of your tenants consistently.
- ☐ Document your reasons for rejecting any applicant.
- ☐ Make sure that all prospective tenants have fully filled out their rental application.
- ☐ Make sure that all of your notices are in writing and always keep copies of every notice given to your tenants.
- ☐ Do not accept partial payments without a signed partial payment agreement.
- ☐ Do not be afraid to inspect your rental property regularly—you own it!
- ☐ Keep tenant files up-to-date, accurate, and thorough.
- ☐ Make sure that you have a responsible maintenance person and that your tenants can reach the person.

Appendix B: Notice Requirements to Terminate a Month-to-Month Tenancy (State by State)

This appendix lists the notice requirements to terminate a month-to-month tenancy. The listed time required is found in each state's statute concerning this notice requirement. N/A means there is no definitive state law.

	To Landlord	To Tenant
Alabama	10 days	10 days
Alaska	30 days	30 days
Arizona	30 days	30 days
Arkansas	10 days	10 days
California	30 days	30 days (60 days in some locations)
Colorado	N/A	N/A
Connecticut	N/A	N/A
Delaware	60 days	60 days
District of Columbia	30 days	30 days
Florida	15 days	15 days
Georgia	60 days	30 days
Hawaii	45 days	28 days

Idaho	a month	a month
Illinois	30 days	30 days
Indiana	a month	a month
Iowa	30 days	30 days
Kansas	30 days	30 days
Kentucky	30 days	30 days
Louisiana	10 days	10 days
Maine	30 days	30 days
Maryland	a month	a month
Massachusetts	time between rent interval or 30 days, whichever is longer	time between rent interval or 30 days, whichever is longer
Michigan	time between payments	time between payments
Minnesota	time between rent interval or 3 months, whichever is less	time between rent interval or 3 months, whichever is less
Mississippi	30 days	30 days
Missouri	a month	a month
Montana	30 days	30 days
Nebraska	30 days	30 days
Nevada	30 days	30 days
New Hampshire	30 days	30 days
New Jersey	N/A	N/A
New Mexico	30 days	30 days
New York	a month	a month

North Carolina	7 days	7 days
North Dakota	30 days	30 days
Ohio	30 days	30 days
Oklahoma	30 days	30 days
Oregon	30 days	30 days
Pennsylvania	N/A	N/A
Rhode Island	30 days	30 days
South Carolina	30 days	30 days
South Dakota	a month	a month
Tennessee	30 days	30 days
Texas	typically, a month	typically, a month
Utah	N/A	N/A
Vermont	30 days	one rental period
Virginia	30 days	30 days
Washington	20 days	30 days
West Virginia	a month	a month
Wisconsin	28 days	28 days
Wyoming	N/A	N/A

Appendix C:

Security Deposit Limits (State by State)

(N/A means there is no definitive state law.)

Alabama	N/A
Alaska	Two month's rent, if rent is up to $2,000 per month
Arizona	One and a half month's rent
Arkansas	Two month's rent
California	From two to three and a half month's rent, depending on the circumstances
Colorado	N/A
Connecticut	Either one or two month's rent, depending on the age of the tenant
Delaware	No more than one month's rent in most circumstances
District of Columbia	One month's rent
Florida	N/A
Georgia	N/A
Hawaii	One month's rent
Idaho	N/A

Illinois	N/A
Indiana	N/A
Iowa	Two month's rent
Kansas	From one to one and a half month's rent, depending on the circumstances
Kentucky	N/A
Louisiana	N/A
Maine	Two month's rent
Maryland	Two month's rent
Massachusetts	One month's rent
Michigan	One and a half month's rent
Minnesota	N/A
Mississippi	N/A
Missouri	Two month's rent
Montana	N/A
Nebraska	From one to one and a half month's rent
Nevada	Three month's rent
New Hampshire	One month's rent or $100, whichever is greater
New Jersey	One and a half month's rent
New Mexico	No more than one month's rent, depending on the type of tenancy
New York	N/A
North Carolina	From one and a half to two month's rent

North Dakota	One month's rent, possibly more for a pet
Ohio	N/A
Oklahoma	N/A
Oregon	N/A
Pennsylvania	No more than two month's rent
Rhode Island	One month's rent
South Carolina	N/A
South Dakota	Normally, one month's rent
Tennessee	N/A
Texas	N/A
Utah	N/A
Vermont	N/A
Virginia	Two month's rent
Washington	N/A
West Virginia	N/A
Wisconsin	N/A
Wyoming	N/A

Appendix D:
Time Frames for Providing Security Deposit Statements (State by State)

(N/A means there is no definitive state law.)

Alabama	N/A
Alaska	Either 14 or 30 days, depending on the tenant's notice to vacate
Arizona	14 days
Arkansas	30 days
California	3 weeks
Colorado	Various limits depending on different factors (consult with counsel)
Connecticut	Either 15 or 30 days, depending on date of receipt of tenant's forwarding address
Delaware	20 days
District of Columbia	45 days
Florida	Between 15 and 60 days, depending on any dispute from the tenant
Georgia	A month

Hawaii	14 days
Idaho	Minimum of 21 days
Illinois	Between 30 and 45 days, depending on any dispute from the tenant
Indiana	45 days
Iowa	30 days
Kansas	30 days
Kentucky	Between 30 and 60 days, depending on any notice of dispute received from the tenant
Louisiana	A month
Maine	Between 21 and 30 days, based on the nature of the tenancy
Maryland	Between 30 and 45 days, based on whether tenant abandoned the property or was evicted
Massachusetts	30 days
Michigan	30 days
Minnesota	Between 5 days and 3 weeks, based on reason for tenant leaving
Mississippi	45 days
Missouri	30 days
Montana	Either 10 or 30 days, depending on the deductions
Nebraska	14 days
Nevada	30 days
New Hampshire	30 days

New Jersey	Generally 30 days, less if tenant forced to evacuate
New Mexico	30 days
New York	Reasonable time frame
North Carolina	30 days
North Dakota	30 days
Ohio	30 days
Oklahoma	30 days
Oregon	31 days
Pennsylvania	30 days
Rhode Island	20 days
South Carolina	30 days
South Dakota	Minimum of 2 weeks, can be up to 45 days
Tennessee	N/A
Texas	30 days
Utah	Either 15 or 30 days, depending on date of receipt of tenant's forwarding address
Vermont	14 days
Virginia	45 days
Washington	14 days
West Virginia	N/A
Wisconsin	N/A
Wyoming	As few as 15 or as many as 60 days, depending on damage and date of receipt of tenant's forwarding address

Appendix E: Time Permitted for Rent to be Paid after Nonpayment of Rent Notice (State by State)

(N/A means there is no definitive state law.)

Alabama	Landlord only needs to give unconditional quit notice before eviction
Alaska	7 days
Arizona	5 days
Arkansas	Tenant must be 6 months in arrears prior to an action for possession
California	3 days
Colorado	3 days
Connecticut	9 days
Delaware	5 days
District of Columbia	30 days
Florida	3 days
Georgia	Landlord can file for eviction immediately if is rent not paid when due
Hawaii	5 days

Idaho	3 days
Illinois	5 days
Indiana	10 days
Iowa	3 days
Kansas	Depends on the length of the tenancy
Kentucky	7 days
Louisiana	Landlord only needs to give unconditional quit notice before eviction
Maine	7 days
Maryland	5 days
Massachusetts	Depends on tenant's status (lease agreement or holdover)
Michigan	7 days
Minnesota	14 days
Mississippi	3 days
Missouri	Landlord only needs to give unconditional quit notice before eviction
Montana	3 days
Nebraska	3 days
Nevada	5 days
New Hampshire	7 days
New Jersey	30 days
New Mexico	3 days
New York	Minimum of 3 days (look to lease)

North Carolina	10 days
North Dakota	Landlord only needs to give unconditional quit notice before eviction
Ohio	Landlord only needs to give unconditional quit notice before eviction
Oklahoma	5 days
Oregon	Either 3 or 6 days (look to lease)
Pennsylvania	10 days
Rhode Island	5 days
South Carolina	5 days, but may be able to evict immediately based on the lease
South Dakota	If 3 days late, landlord only needs to give unconditional quit notice before eviction
Tennessee	14 days
Texas	No statute
Utah	3 days
Vermont	14 days
Virginia	5 days
Washington	3 days
West Virginia	Landlord only needs to give unconditional quit notice before eviction
Wisconsin	Varies based on the type of tenancy
Wyoming	3 days

Appendix F:
Notice Requirements for Landlord to Access the Dwelling (Nonemergency) (State by State)

(N/A means there is no definitive state law.)

Alabama	N/A
Alaska	24 hours
Arizona	2 days
Arkansas	N/A
California	24 hours
Colorado	N/A
Connecticut	Reasonable notice
Delaware	48 hours
District of Columbia	N/A
Florida	12 hours
Georgia	N/A
Hawaii	2 days
Idaho	N/A
Illinois	N/A
Indiana	N/A

Iowa	24 hours
Kansas	Reasonable notice
Kentucky	2 days
Louisiana	N/A
Maine	24 hours
Maryland	N/A
Massachusetts	N/A
Michigan	N/A
Minnesota	Reasonable notice
Mississippi	N/A
Missouri	N/A
Montana	24 hours
Nebraska	1 day
Nevada	24 hours
New Hampshire	Adequate notice
New Jersey	N/A
New Mexico	24 hours
New York	N/A
North Carolina	N/A
North Dakota	Reasonable notice
Ohio	24 hours
Oklahoma	1 day
Oregon	24 hours
Pennsylvania	N/A

Rhode Island	2 days
South Carolina	24 hours
South Dakota	N/A
Tennessee	N/A
Texas	N/A
Utah	N/A
Vermont	48 hours
Virginia	24 hours
Washington	2 days
West Virginia	N/A
Wisconsin	Reasonable notice
Wyoming	N/A

Appendix G:

States that Allow
a Tenant
to "Repair and Deduct"

Alaska	Missouri
Arizona	Montana
California	Nebraska
Connecticut	Nevada
Delaware	New York
Hawaii	North Dakota
Iowa	Oklahoma
Kentucky	Oregon
Louisiana	Rhode Island
Maine	South Dakota
Massachusetts	Tennessee
Michigan	Texas
Minnesota	Vermont
Mississippi	Washington

Appendix H:
States that Allow Tenants to Withhold Rent for Failure to Provide Essential Services

Alaska

Arizona

California

Connecticut

Delaware

District of Columbia

Florida

Hawaii

Illinois

Iowa

Kansas

Kentucky

Maine

Maryland

Massachusetts

Michigan

Minnesota

Missouri

Montana

Nebraska

Nevada

New Hampshire

New Jersey

New Mexico

New York

Ohio

Oklahoma

Oregon

Pennsylvania

Rhode Island

South Carolina

South Dakota

Tennessee

Vermont

Virginia

Washington

Wisconsin

Wyoming

Appendix I:

Sample Forms

This appendix provides some samples of additional forms or letters you may need. Your situation will be unique, making a blank form not particularly helpful (except for the Partial Payment Agreement), but having an example will help you craft your own document.

Application Rejection Letter

Date: April 30, 2006

Dear Applicant,

After reviewing your application for residency, I regret to inform you that your application for tenancy has been rejected for the following reason(s).

The amount of the monthly rent is a higher percentage of your gross income than is financially acceptable. The monthly rent represents 35% of your monthly gross income, and the property only accepts prospective applicants if the monthly rent is 28% or less of the applicant's gross monthly income.

If you have any questions or concerns, please do not hesitate to contact our office.

Sincerely,

Larry Landlord

Larry Landlord

Landlord's Permission to Sublet

Larry Landlord and Tommy Tenant hereby agree, for the property commonly known as 123 Main Street, Ourtown, MO 55555, to the following terms of subleasing:

1. Landlord grants permission to the above-named tenant to sublease the premises listed above to a sublessee for the period beginning on the 1st day of July, 2006, and ending on the 30th day of April, 2007.

2. Tenant agrees that the sublessee shall conform to all obligations and covenants described in the original lease between landlord and tenant.

3. Any and all adult sublessees shall complete a credit application and must meet the normal financial and other criteria required for tenancy.

4. In the event that legal action is necessary to enforce the term of this or the original lease, the prevailing party is entitled to its attorney's fees.

5. Tenant agrees and understands that this sublet agreement in no way releases tenant from any obligation set forth in the original lease.

This agreement is entered into this 30th day of June, 2006.

Landlord *Larry Landlord*

Tenant *Tommy Tenant*

Appendix J:

Blank Forms

This appendix contains some of the most common forms a landlord needs. Each form can be removed from these pages and filled in for immediate use. Make a photocopy of the page prior to writing on it, so you can maintain a clean, blank document to use again and again.

Each of these forms is also available on the attached CD-ROM. The CD-ROM is compatible with both PC and Mac formats. A listing of the forms is contained on the CD-ROM to help you select the file you need.

Once selected, you can easily complete the form directly on your computer. Simply fill in the missing information. You can then have a document that is completely computer-generated and ready to be signed. You can, of course, also just print the blank forms from the disc and fill them in as you would the forms in the book.

Landlord to Tenant Forms

Tenant to Landlord Forms

TENANT APPLICATION

PERSONAL DATA

Name of Tenant: _____ Date of Birth: _____/_____/_____

Phone No: _____

SSN: _____ Driv. Lic. #: _____ Expiration Date: _____/_____/_____

Name of Co-Tenant: _____ Date of Birth: _____/_____/_____

SSN: _____ Driv. Lic. #: _____ Expiration Date: _____/_____/_____

Present Address: _____

Time at Present Address: _____

Landlord Name: _____ Landlord Phone: _____

OTHER OCCUPANTS:

Name: _____ Date of Birth: _____/_____/_____ SSN: _____

Relationship: _____

Name: _____ Date of Birth: _____/_____/_____ SSN: _____

Relationship: _____

Name: _____ Date of Birth: _____/_____/_____ SSN: _____

Relationship: _____

Name: _____ Date of Birth: _____/_____/_____ SSN: _____

Relationship: _____

Pets (No more than _____ dogs allowed):

Type: _____ Weight: _____ Color: _____

Name: _____

Type: _____ Weight: _____ Color: _____

Name: _____

Type: _____ Weight: _____ Color: _____

Name: _____

Car Make: _____ Model: _____ Year: _____
Color: _____ License Plate: _____

Current Employer	Former Employer
Address	Address
Phone Number	Phone Number
Position	Position
Salary	Salary

Have you ever filed a petition for bankruptcy? _____

Have you ever been evicted from any tenancy? _____

Have you ever willfully and intentionally refused to pay any rent when due? _____

Have you ever been taken to court for not paying your rent? _____

Have you ever been convicted of a crime? _____

If you answered yes to any of these questions, please give details:

I declare, under penalty of perjury, that the foregoing is true and correct. I also agree to provide a photocopy of the title of the mobile I am planning to move into the park prior to moving in, and acknowledge that I have no right to move in without providing it.

Tenant (Print Name) _____

Tenant (Signature) _____ Date _____/_____/_____

RESIDENTIAL LEASE AGREEMENT

This agreement is made this ____ day of _____, 200__, by and between _____,
Lessor, and _____, Lessee(s), and is for the premises commonly known as
_____.

Said premises is furnished/unfurnished, and contains:

Witnesseth: that for and in consideration of the payment of rent as called for herein, and of the performance of
the covenants herein, the Lessor does hereby lease to the Lessee, and the Lessee does lease from the Lessor the
above described property.

1) <u>Term:</u> The term of the lease shall be for a period of _____ months and shall commence on
the _____ day of _____, 200____ and shall continue until the _____ day
of _____, 200____. Lessee shall pay $_____ for the term of the
lease as follows:

      In advance, on, or before the 1st Day of each month commence the _____ day of _____
_____, 200____, an installment of $_____ and additional installments of
$_____, on or before the 1st day of each month thereafter.

2) <u>Security:</u> A security deposit in the total amount of $_____ has been paid in full and lessor hereby
acknowledges receipt of $_____, as and for the security deposit. All but $_____ of the security
deposit shall be refundable upon expiration of the lease, subject to Landlord's offsets for cleaning and damages in
excess of $_____. The deposit shall not serve as last month's rent, and rent for that month shall be
paid as set forth above.

3) It is further agreed and understood that rent shall not be prorated on a daily basis, and rent when due, is due
and payable for the entire month.

4) <u>Occupancy:</u> It is further agreed that occupancy is to limited to no more than _____ adults and _____
children; that all utilities are to be paid by the Lessee, and Lessee has the utilities placed in Lessee's name.

5) <u>Pets:</u> Pets shall not be allowed under this agreement and any change shall require the written consent of the
Lessor.

6) <u>Sublet/Assignment:</u> Lessee shall not sublet said premises or any part thereof or assign or pledge this agreement
without the prior written consent of Lessor.

7) <u>Termination</u>: Upon expiration of this agreement the Lessee shall peacefully surrender the premises to the Lessor in as good a condition as when received, normal wear excepted.

8) <u>Maintenance</u>: Lessee shall maintain the premises in a clean and sanitary condition at all times, and in such manner as to not be offensive to the senses or damaging to the property, as judged by the Lessor. Lessee shall water and maintain all plants immediately adjacent to the outside of the unit. Lessee shall be responsible for pest control.

9) <u>Alterations:</u> Lessee shall make no alteration, addition, or improvement to the premises inside or outside without the prior written consent of Lessor.

10) <u>Repairs</u>: Lessee acknowledges that all appliances are in good working order and Lessee shall effectuate all repairs to fixtures, coolers, and premises as needed that stem from the misuse or negligence of the Lessee. In no event shall the Lessor be responsible for repairs, service, maintenance, or damages occasioned by the negligence or willful misuse by the Lessee, and costs advanced upon behalf of the Lessee by Lessor shall accrue as rent to be paid with the regular rent on or before the day rent is next due. Lessee acknowledges that the premises are fit and habitable and that there are no outstanding or unperformed requests for repair.

11) <u>Encumbrances</u>: Lessee agrees to not encumber or cause any encumbrance or lien of any sort to be placed upon the title to the property and agrees to indemnify Lessor for the costs of any action, whether commercial or legal, to clear such encumbrances or liens. Further, the occurrence of a lien or encumbrance brought about through the action of Lessee shall constitute grounds for breach of lease, and Lessor may terminate the lease agreement. Any amounts advanced by Lessor to remove an encumbrance or lien shall be considered unpaid rent and the same shall be due from Lessee to Lessor immediately, without demand.

12) <u>Conduct:</u> The Lessee(s) shall conduct themselves, and require their guests on the premises likewise to conduct themselves, in a manner that will not interfere with the peaceful and quiet enjoyment of the neighboring premises.

13) <u>Tenancy:</u> Upon expiration of the term required by this agreement, the agreement shall continue in full force and effect on a month-to-month basis, reserving the right of both parties to terminate the agreement with a 30-day notice, as required by law. Lessor may increase the amount of monthly rent next due after expiration of the lease term by giving written notice 30 days prior to the last day of the lease. Subsequent rent increases shall be at the discretion of the landlord, subject to the legal requirements of law. Nothing in this paragraph shall preclude the parties from voluntarily entering into a new agreement or extending this lease agreement.

14) <u>Breach:</u> Failure to pay rent or other lawful charges when due, or to comply with any other provision of this lease or applicable Landlord/Tenant law, shall constitute an immediate and material breach, and the injured party, may, upon service of such notice as is required by law, terminate the lease.

15) <u>Forfeiture/Default/Costs:</u> The security deposit will be returned upon termination of this agreement and upon the surrender by Lessee of the entire premises, subject to inspection of Lessor, and upon a finding that there is no damage by reason of the acts of Lessee, guests, and invitees, nor any other material noncompliance or unfilled obligation of Lessee relating to this lease, and further providing that there is no outstanding rent due or financial obligation as called for, either expressly or impliedly by this agreement or the operation of law. In the event Lessee unilaterally terminates the lease prior to the expiration of its term, the deposit shall be forfeited. In all other cases, Lessor may use all or part of the deposit as an offset for cleaning, repairs, and damage, over and above normal wear and tear occasioned by the tenancy.

16) <u>Attorney Fees:</u> In the event of a breach or other dispute, the prevailing party shall be entitled to its reasonable costs and attorney's fees.

17) <u>Subordination:</u> This agreement is and shall remain subordinate to any encumbrance now existing or hereafter placed upon the residence by operation of law or by Lessor.

18) <u>Notices and Payment:</u> All notices shall be made in writing and delivered or mailed. In the case of the Lessor, to: _____; in the case of the Lessee, to the address of the premises. Rent shall be payable at the Lessor's address, by mail or in person.

19) <u>Partial Payment:</u> Partial payment of rent is not acceptable, and tender and acceptance by Lessor shall not constitute waiver of Lessor's rights, nor shall acceptance serve to create a course of dealing between the parties.

20) <u>Payments/NSF Checks:</u> Rent is due and payable on the first day of each month. If any installment is late, the Lessee shall be in breach and owner shall be entitled to terminate this agreement for nonpayment of rent. Rent tendered and accepted after the 5th day of the month shall be subject to, and include, a late charge of $ _____.00. A charge of $ _____.00 will be imposed for any and all checks returned by the bank for reasons of insufficient funds or closed account. Imposition of this charge shall not preclude Lessor from seeking any and all other remedies that may be available at law.

21) <u>Access:</u> Lessor reserves the right to enter the premises at reasonable times and upon reasonable notice to Lessee in order to inspect, make necessary repairs, supply service to the Lessee, or show it to prospective purchasers, lien holders, contractors, or health or building inspectors, or other public officials in the course of their public duties. A 48-hour notice shall be given to Lessee in the normal course of events. Lessee agrees to make the premises available to Lessor to effect repairs and waives notice in case of emergency.

22) <u>Keys:</u> Lessee acknowledges the receipt of two door keys. Lessee agrees to reimburse Lessor for all costs associated with the loss of keys by Lessee. Upon the expiration of the agreement, Lessee agrees to return the keys, and in lieu thereof, pay all costs and consequential damages associated with the replacement thereof.

23) <u>Binding Effect:</u> This agreement shall be binding upon and inure to the benefit of the heirs, executors, administrators, successors and assigns of the Lessor and Lessee, except as specifically noted.

24) <u>Amendment:</u> The terms, conditions, responsibilities, obligations, rights, duties, and privileges created or called for under this lease may be modified only by a writing signed by both parties.

25) <u>Lead-Based Paint Disclosure:</u> Tenant acknowledges receipt of the required Lead-Based Paint disclosure.

Lessee, by initialing, acknowledges receipt of a copy of this agreement.

_____   _____
Lessee   Lessor

_____/_____/_____   _____/_____/_____
Date   Date

APPLICANT'S AUTHORIZATION TO RELEASE RECORDS

TO: _____

[NAME OF BUSINESS OR INSTITUTION WHERE INFORMATION IS REQUESTED]

I, _____, AUTHORIZE _____

[NAME OF TENANT]   *[NAME OF LANDLORD]*

TO BE ABLE TO OBTAIN ANY PERTINENT CREDIT, EMPLOYMENT, BANKING, OR RESIDENCE INFOR-MATION AS IS NECESSARY IN CONJUNCTION WITH MY PENDING APPLICATION FOR RESIDENCY. I HEREBY AUTHORIZE THE RELEASE OF THOSE RECORDS TO THE LANDLORD NAMED ABOVE. I EXPRESSLY AGREE TO WAIVE ANY PRIVILEGES WITH RESPECT TO ANY INFORMATION RELEASED TO THE LANDLORD NAMED ABOVE.

APPLICANT _____

DATE _____

This page intentionally left blank.

DISCLOSURE OF INFORMATION ON LEAD-BASED PAINT
AND/OR
LEAD-BASED PAINT HAZARDS

Lead Warning Statement

Housing built before 1978 may contain lead-based paint. Lead from paint, paint chips, and dust can pose health hazards if not managed properly. Lead exposure is especially harmful to young children and pregnant women. Before renting pre-1978 housing, lessors must disclose the presence of known lead-based paint and/or lead-based paint hazards in the dwelling. Lessees must also receive a federally approved pamphlet on lead poisoning prevention.

Lessor's Disclosure

(a) Presence of lead-based paint and/or lead-based paint hazards (check (1) or (2) below):

   (1) ____ Known lead-based paint and/or lead-based hazards are present in the housing (explain).

   (2) ____ Lessor has no knowledge of lead-based paint and/or lead-based paint hazards in the housing.

(b) Records and reports available to the Lessor (check (1) or (2) below):

   (1) ____ Lessor has provided the Lessee with all available records and reports pertaining to lead-based pain and/or lead-based paint hazards in the housing (list documents).

   (2) ____ Lessor has no reports or records pertaining to lead-based paint and/or lead-based paint hazards in the housing.

Lessee's Acknowledgment (initial)

(c) ____ Lessee has received copies of all information listed above.

(d) ____ Lessee has received the pamphlet *Protect Your Family from Lead in Your Home.*

Agent's Acknowledgment (initial)

(e) ____ Agent has informed the Lessor of the Lessor's obligations under 42 U.S.C. 4852.

(f) ____ and is aware of his/her responsibility to ensure compliance.

Certification of Accuracy

The following parties have reviewed the information above and certify, to the best of their knowledge, that the information they have provided is true and accurate.

Lessor: _____ Date: _____

Lessee: _____ Date: _____

Agent: _____ Date: _____

This page intentionally left blank.

MOVE-IN/MOVE-OUT INSPECTION FORM

Property Address: _____

Date of Move-In: _____ Date of Move-Out: _____

	<u>Condition on Arrival</u>	<u>Condition on Departure</u>

Living Room
Floor Coverings

Walls

Windows/Screens

Doors/Locks

Fireplace/Chimney

Light Fixtures

Ceiling/Roof

Other

Dining Room
Floor Coverings

Walls

Windows/Screens

Fireplace/Chimney

Light Fixtures

Ceiling/Roof

Other

Kitchen
Floor Coverings

Walls

Windows/Screens

	__Condition on Arrival__	__Condition on Departure__
Countertops	_____	_____
Appliances	_____	_____
Cabinets	_____	_____
Light Fixtures	_____	_____
Ceiling/Roof	_____	_____
Other	_____	_____

Bedroom 1

Floor Coverings	_____	_____
Walls	_____	_____
Windows/Screens	_____	_____
Doors/Locks	_____	_____
Fireplace/Chimney	_____	_____
Light Fixtures	_____	_____
Ceiling/Roof	_____	_____
Other	_____	_____

Bedroom 2

Floor Coverings	_____	_____
Walls	_____	_____
Windows/Screens	_____	_____
Doors/Locks	_____	_____
Fireplace/Chimney	_____	_____
Light Fixtures	_____	_____
Ceiling/Roof	_____	_____
Other	_____	_____

	Condition on Arrival	Condition on Departure
Bathroom		
Floor Coverings	_____	_____
Walls	_____	_____
Windows/Screens	_____	_____
Doors/Locks	_____	_____
Tub/Shower	_____	_____
Light Fixtures	_____	_____
Ceiling/Roof	_____	_____
Countertops	_____	_____
Other	_____	_____
Other Areas		
Air Conditioning	_____	_____
Heating System	_____	_____
Front Yard	_____	_____
Swimming Pool	_____	_____
Jacuzzi/Hot Tub	_____	_____
Attic	_____	_____
Basement	_____	_____
Garage	_____	_____
Smoke Detector	_____	_____
Other	_____	_____
	_____	_____
	_____	_____
	_____	_____

This page intentionally left blank.

MAINTENANCE REQUEST FORM

DATE: _____

TIME: _____

RESIDENT NAME: _____

RESIDENT ADDRESS: _____

RESIDENT PHONE NUMBER: _____

SPECIFY NATURE OF PROBLEM: _____

_____

_____

_____

DATE OF SCHEDULED REPAIR: _____

DATE REPAIR COMPLETED: _____

This page intentionally left blank.

NOTICE OF TERMINATION OF TENANCY (NONPAYMENT OF RENT)

TO: _____   DATE: _____

_____

_____

FROM: _____

PROPERTY ADDRESS: _____

This is to provide you notice that your tenancy at the above property will be terminated for nonpayment of rent unless all outstanding rents and other amounts owed, in the amount of $ _____, are tendered prior to the expiration of _____ days from the date of receipt of this notice. Monthly rent is $ _____.

$ _____   Rent for _____

$ _____   Late Charge

$ _____   Other: _____

$ _____   Total owed

You have _____ days from date of receipt, or no more than _____ days from date of mailing, to pay or vacate the premises. Should you fail to abide by this notice, legal action will be brought to regain possession. Please arrange to pay or to vacate and surrender the premises and keys in the time allowed.

Payment or surrender should be made to:_____

Tenant: _____

Sent by: Certified mail, #_____, on _____.

This page intentionally left blank.

NOTICE OF TERMINATION OF MONTH-TO-MONTH TENANCY

Date: _____

To: _____ , Tenant

From: _____ , Landlord

Re: 30-day Notice to Terminate Tenancy

Dear Tenant:

This is to inform you that management has decided to terminate your month-to-month tenancy as of _____, 200_____. As a 30-day notice is required to terminate a tenancy, this is your notification that your tenancy shall terminate on _____, 200_____.

Pursuant to your rental agreement, rent for the upcoming month will still be due, and rent must be paid if you choose to remain in possession for the month. Your security deposit is not prepaid rent.

In the event that you fail to vacate as requested, an action for possession of the premises will be timely brought by your landlord, and in addition to any other remedy at law, damages may be sought.

You are invited to arrange a move-out inspection and are asked to provide a forwarding address to which the security deposit disposition may be sent, along with a refund or statement of additional charges, if any.

Sincerely,

_____

This page intentionally left blank.

NOTICE OF NONRENEWAL

Date: _____

To: _____ , Tenant

From: _____ , Landlord

Re: Notice of Nonrenewal

Dear Tenant:

This is to inform you that your tenancy will not be renewed at the end of the present term. Therefore, you will need to vacate on or before the last day of the lease, the _____ day of _____, 200____.

In the event that you fail to vacate as requested, an action for possession of the premises will be brought in a timely manner by your landlord, and in addition to any other remedy at law, damages may be sought.

You are invited to arrange a move-out inspection and are asked to provide a forwarding address to which the security deposit disposition may be sent, along with a refund or statement of additional charges, if any.

Sincerely,

_____

This page intentionally left blank.

NOTICE OF CHANGE IN OWNERSHIP

TO: _____

THIS NOTICE IS TO ADVISE YOU OF A CHANGE IN OWNERSHIP FOR THE PROPERTY THAT YOU CURRENTLY OCCUPY. THE NEW OWNER'S NAME IS _____, AND THE ADDRESS OF THE NEW OWNER IS _____.

DIRECT ALL RENTAL PAYMENTS, INQUIRIES, OR QUESTIONS FROM _____ FORWARD TO THE NEW OWNER'S ADDRESS. INFORMATION REGARDING YOUR SECURITY DEPOSIT WILL BE FORWARDED AS APPROPRIATE. FEEL FREE TO CONTACT US IF YOU HAVE ANY QUESTIONS OR CONCERNS IN THE MEANTIME.

SINCERELY,

_____

CURRENT OWNER

This page intentionally left blank.

NOTICE OF MATERIAL BREACH
(LANDLORD TO TENANT)

Date: _____

To: _____ , Tenant

From: _____ , Landlord

Re: Notice of Material Breach

Dear Tenant:

This is to inform you that you are in material breach of your rental agreement, and the rental agreement will terminate in _____ days if the breach is not remedied in _____ days. The nature of the breach is as follows:

If you do not remedy the breach within the time specified in this notice, an action for possession of the premises will be brought and all damages relating to the breach will be sought.

Sincerely,

_____

This page intentionally left blank.

NOTICE OF LANDLORD'S INTENT TO ENTER THE PREMISES

Date: _____

To: _____ , Tenant

From: _____ , Landlord

Re: Intent to Enter the Premises

Dear Tenant:

This is to inform you that the landlord intends to enter the premises on the _____ day of _____,
200_____, at the approximate time of _____a.m./p.m., in order to:

We thank you in advance for your cooperation.

Sincerely,

_____

This page intentionally left blank.

RENTAL AGREEMENT ADDENDUM

This addendum is made this ___ day of _____, 200___, by and between _____,
Landlord, and _____, Tenant, and is intended as a supplement to the lease between the parties dated the ___ day of _____, 200___.

The parties agree as follows:

_____   _____
Landlord   Tenant

Date: _____   Date: _____

This page intentionally left blank.

NOTICE OF MATERIAL AND IRREPARABLE BREACH
(LANDLORD TO TENANT)

Date: _____

To: _____, Tenant

From: _____, Landlord

RE: Notice of Immediate Termination

Dear _____:

Please be advised that management has chosen to terminate your tenancy and right to possession, immediately. An action for possession will be filed in order to enforce the right to termination. You may voluntarily surrender the premises by vacating immediately.

This action is being taken for the reason that you have committed a material and irreparable breach, to wit:

Please arrange to vacate the premises immediately. Upon receipt of a forwarding address and request for disposition, your security deposit, if any, will be accounted for.

Sincerely,

_____

This page intentionally left blank.

NOTICE FOR NONCOMPLIANCE MATERIALLY AFFECTING HEALTH AND SAFETY

Date: _____

To: _____ , Tenant

From: _____ , Landlord

Property: _____

This is to inform you that you are in noncompliance with your rental agreement on the above property, which materially affects health and safety. This noncompliance stems from the following prohibited activity:

You have _____ days from the date of this notice to completely cure the violation. If you fail to completely cure, a *Forcible Entry and Detainer Action* will be commenced to recover possession of the property and damages will be sought.

Be advised that if there is a subsequent breach of a same or similar nature within the term of your leasehold or any extension thereof, the management may elect to terminate your occupancy after receipt of the notice of that breach.

Sincerely,

_____

This page intentionally left blank.

PARTIAL PAYMENT AGREEMENT

The management of _____ agrees to accept partial payment in the amount
of $ _____ from _____, tenant(s)
occupying the following dwelling: _____.

After accepting the partial payment described herein, a balance of $_____ remains. Late
charges accrue at $_____ per diem.

The balance of the rent is currently due and owed and will be paid in full by the ____ day of _____,
200___.

By signing this partial payment agreement, tenant promises that if the remaining rent, late charges, and other fees
are not paid in full by the date agreed to above, the landlord retains the right to terminate the rental agreement,
and tenant will be liable for all additional costs incurred and any other relief allowable under the laws of this state.

Dated this _____ day of _____, 200___.

_____   _____
Landlord   Tenant

This page intentionally left blank.

NOTICE OF ABANDONMENT

Date: _____

To: _____ , Tenant

From: _____ , Landlord

Re: Property located at _____

Your dwelling unit is believed to be abandoned. Based on the information available, it appears that you are absent without notice to the landlord, and the rent on the dwelling remains unpaid. There is no reasonable evidence, other than the presence of your personal property, that you continue to occupy the dwelling.

If you intend to remain in possession, please contact the undersigned immediately to inform us that you have not abandoned the dwelling. If we do not hear from you in the requisite time frame, we will retake possession of the dwelling, consistent with the laws of this state.

Sincerely,

_____

This page intentionally left blank.

SECURITY DEPOSIT ITEMIZATION

Date: _____

To: _____ , Tenant

From: _____ , Landlord

Property Address: _____

Term of Tenancy: _____

1. Security Deposit of $_____ was received on _____

2. Interest on Deposit (if required by law or rental agreement) _____

3. Tenant security deposit credit (sum of 1 and 2) $ _____

4. Repairs, replacements, cleaning, and other losses and costs associated with tenancy:

1)_____ Amount: _____

2)_____ Amount: _____

3)_____ Amount: _____

4)_____ Amount: _____

5)_____ Amount: _____

Total: $ _____

5. After applying Tenant's security deposit to the total amount due under line 4:

☐ Landlord owes tenant $ _____

☐ Tenant owes landlord $ _____

COMMENTS:

_____

_____

_____

This page intentionally left blank.

FORCIBLE DETAINER (EVICTION) COMPLAINT FORM
(NONPAYMENT)

Plaintiff _____

Plaintiff's address _____

IN THE _____ COURT OF THE STATE OF _____
IN AND FOR THE COUNTY OF _____

_____,)	
Plaintiff,)	
)	
)	
vs.)	No.
)	
_____,)	COMPLAINT
Defendant,)	(FORCIBLE DETAINER)

Comes now the Plaintiff, and for its cause of action, alleges and states the following:

I.

That the Plaintiff owns the premises located at _____ [address], County of _____, State of _____. The Defendants rented the property pursuant to a rental agreement (lease) with the Plaintiff. Jurisdiction and venue are proper in this Court.

II.

Pursuant to the rental agreement, monthly rent is payable on the 1st day of each calendar month in the amount of $_____ with a late charge of $_____ per month if payment is not received by the _____.

III.

Defendant(s) failed to tender rent for the month of_____, and appropriate notice was delivered in person on _____, requesting tender of rent or vacation and surrender of the premises. Rent in the amount of $_____ and late charges of $_____ for _____ has not been tendered to date. This action is brought pursuant to statute, and this matter sounds in contract.

IV.

The daily rent is $_____ a day and would commence on _____.

WHEREFORE Plaintiff prays for Judgment and relief as follows:

1) For a determination that the Defendant(s) are guilty of Forcible Detainer;
2) For an order of the court directing restitution of the premises to the Plaintiff;
3) For a judgment for such rent as the court may find due and owing up to and through the date of restoration or vacation of the premises;
4) For the costs of this action as the court may deem reasonable under the circumstances;
5) Such other relief as the court may deem fair and equitable under the circumstances.

Dated this _____ day of _____, 200_____.

_____
Plaintiff

FORCIBLE DETAINER (EVICTION) COMPLAINT FORM
(NONCOMPLIANCE)

Plaintiff _____

Plaintiff's address _____

IN THE _____ COURT OF THE STATE OF _____
IN AND FOR THE COUNTY OF _____

_____,)	
Plaintiff,)	
)	
)	
vs.)	No.
)	
_____,)	COMPLAINT
Defendant,)	(FORCIBLE DETAINER)

Comes now the Plaintiff, and for its cause of action, alleges and states the following:

I.

That the Plaintiff owns the premises located at _____ [address], County of _____, State of _____. The Defendants rented the property pursuant to a rental agreement (lease) with the Plaintiff. Jurisdiction and venue are proper in this Court.

II.

Pursuant to the rental agreement, the Defendant(s) were obligated to comply with the terms and conditions contained in the rental agreement (lease) between the parties.

III.

The defendant(s) has violated the terms and conditions of the agreement between the parties by engaging in the following prohibited activity:

Appropriate notice was delivered to the defendant(s), and this action followed. This action is brought pursuant to statute, and this matter sounds in contract.

WHEREFORE Plaintiff prays for Judgment and relief as follows:

1) For a determination that the Defendant(s) are guilty of Forcible Detainer;
2) For an order of the court directing restitution of the premises to the Plaintiff;
3) For a judgment for such rent and/or damages as the court may find due and owing up to and through the date of restoration or vacation of the premises;
4) For the costs of this action as the court may deem reasonable under the circumstances;
5) Such other relief as the court may deem fair and equitable under the circumstances.

Dated this _____ day of _____, 200_____.

_____
Plaintiff

COMPLAINT FOR DAMAGES
(POST-JUDGMENT)

Plaintiff _____

Plaintiff's address _____

      IN THE _____ COURT OF THE STATE OF _____

             IN AND FOR THE COUNTY OF _____

_____,	)	
Plaintiff,	)	
	)	
	)	
vs.	)	No.
	)	
_____,	)	COMPLAINT
Defendant,	)	

Comes now the Plaintiff, and for its cause of action, alleges and states the following:

I.

That the Plaintiff owns the premises located at _____ [address], County of _____, State of _____. The Defendant(s) rented the property pursuant to a rental agreement (lease) with the Plaintiff. Jurisdiction and venue are proper in this Court.

II.

Subsequent to the expiration of the tenancy, Plaintiff has sustained damages to the dwelling in excess of the Defendant(s) security deposit. Those damages total $_____. Copies of the documents demonstrating those damages are attached as Exhibits to this Complaint. Plaintiff is entitled to interest at the statutory rate.

170

WHEREFORE Plaintiff prays for Judgment and relief as follows:

1) For a determination that the Plaintiff is entitled to judgment for such sums as the court may find due and owing from the Defendant(s) in this matter;

2) For the costs of this action as the court may deem reasonable under the circumstances along with accruing interest;

3) Such other relief as the court may deem fair and equitable under the circumstances.

Dated this _____ day of _____, 200_____.

_____

Plaintiff

NOTICE OF TERMINATION OF MONTH-TO-MONTH TENANCY
(TENANT TO LANDLORD)

Date: _____

To: _____ , Landlord

From: _____ , Tenant

Re: 30-day Notice to Terminate Tenancy

Dear Landlord:

This is to inform you that we have decided to terminate our month-to-month tenancy as of _____, 200_____. As a 30-day notice is required to terminate a tenancy, this is your notification that our tenancy shall terminate on _____, 200_____.

We will make arrangements to be present at the move-out inspection and will provide our forwarding address, to which the security deposit disposition may be sent.

Sincerely,

_____

This page intentionally left blank.

NOTICE OF MATERIAL BREACH
(TENANT TO LANDLORD)

Date: _____

To: _____ , Landlord

From: _____ , Tenant

Re: Notice of Material Breach

Dear Landlord:

This is to inform you that you are in material breach of our rental agreement, and the rental agreement will terminate in _____ days if the breach is not remedied in _____ days. The nature of the breach is as follows:

If you do not remedy the breach within the time specified in this notice, the rental agreement will terminate and the premises will be vacated.

Sincerely,

_____

Index

M

maintenance, 17, 24, 29, 38, 42, 45, 47, 49, 54, 60

material breach, 51, 52, 53, 54, 69, 72, 73, 86

material noncompliance, 70, 71, 72
   notices for, 72

military personnel, 61, 88

minors, 21

modifications, 8–12, 21, 67, 86

mold, 40, 42

money judgment, 75

month-to-month, 15, 16, 20, 21, 22, 35, 72

move-in inspection, 25, 26, 59, 86, 87

move-out inspection, 17, 59, 60, 87

N

National Center for Environmental Health, 42

national origin, 9, 85

necessities, 21

noise, 70

noncompliance, 18, 19, 34, 45, 69, 70, 71, 72

O

occupants, 17, 19, 37, 58, 70, 73

older structures, 44

oppressive, 1, 16

oral agreements, 15, 18

P

parking, 12, 16, 34

partial payment agreement, 35

passive activity, 78

payroll, 80

peaceful and quiet enjoyment, 20, 44, 52, 70, 73

personal liability coverage, 48

pets, 3, 4, 7, 17, 18, 21 70

probate court, 60, 61

process servers, 73

property coverage, 48

property manager, 17, 33, 48, 69, 71

prostitution, 68, 69, 73

Q

quiet enjoyment, 20, 44, 52, 70, 73

R

race, 2, 9, 85

radon, 40, 43

raising, 35

recording, 76

references, 4, 5

rejection letter, 7

religion, 2, 9, 85

rent, 2, 3, 4, 7, 8, 9, 10, 12, 16, 17, 18, 20, 22, 23, 27, 28, 29, 31, 32, 33, 34, 35, 36, 37, 39, 40, 49, 51, 52, 54, 55, 56, 58, 61, 63, 66, 70, 73, 74, 76, 84, 87, 88

About the Author

As an attorney and author, **James A. Landon** is an energetic and enterprising member of Southern Arizona's legal community.

Landon graduated from the University of Arizona College of Law in 1996, after receiving his Bachelor of Fine Arts, *Cum Laude*, from the University of Arizona. Landon has practiced law in Tucson since 1996, successfully handling thousands of landlord and tenant related cases. He currently practices law as a partner in The Law Offices of Sipe and Landon, a full service law firm located in Tucson.

Always relishing the art of public speaking, Landon made his first television and radio appearances at the age of 10 as a student advocate for the Austin, Texas Independent School District.

Landon was born in Summit, New Jersey, but has lived in Arizona since 1982. He met his wife Heidi while surfing the Internet, and has been married since 1998. The couple has two cats and a beloved dachshund, Vegas.

SPHINX® PUBLISHING'S STATE TITLES
Up-to-Date for Your State

California Titles

How to File for Divorce in CA (4E)	$26.95
How to Settle & Probate an Estate in CA (2E)	$28.95
How to Start a Business in CA (2E)	$21.95
How to Win in Small Claims Court in CA (2E)	$18.95
The Landlord's Legal Guide in CA (2E)	$24.95
Make Your Own CA Will	$18.95
Tenants' Rights in CA	$21.95

Florida Titles

How to File for Divorce in FL (8E)	$28.95
How to Form a Corporation in FL (6E)	$24.95
How to Form a Limited Liability Co. in FL (3E)	$24.95
How to Form a Partnership in FL	$22.95
How to Make a FL Will (7E)	$16.95
How to Probate and Settle an Estate in FL (5E)	$26.95
How to Start a Business in FL (7E)	$21.95
How to Win in Small Claims Court in FL (7E)	$18.95
Land Trusts in Florida (6E)	$29.95
Landlords' Rights and Duties in FL (9E)	$22.95

Georgia Titles

How to File for Divorce in GA (5E)	$21.95
How to Make a GA Will (4E)	$16.95
How to Start a Business in Georgia (3E)	$21.95

Illinois Titles

Child Custody, Visitation and Support in IL	$24.95
How to File for Divorce in IL (3E)	$24.95
How to Make an IL Will (3E)	$16.95
How to Start a Business in IL (4E)	$21.95
The Landlord's Legal Guide in IL	$24.95

Maryland, Virginia and the District of Columbia Titles

How to File for Divorce in MD, VA and DC	$28.95
How to Start a Business in MD, VA or DC	$21.95

Massachusetts Titles

How to Form a Corporation in MA	$24.95
How to Make a MA Will (2E)	$16.95
How to Start a Business in MA (4E)	$21.95
The Landlord's Legal Guide in MA (2E)	$24.95

Michigan Titles

How to File for Divorce in MI (4E)	$24.95
How to Make a MI Will (3E)	$16.95
How to Start a Business in MI (4E)	$24.95

Minnesota Titles

How to File for Divorce in MN $21.95
How to Form a Corporation in MN $24.95
How to Make a MN Will (2E) $16.95

New Jersey Titles

How to File for Divorce in NJ $24.95
How to Start a Business in NJ $21.95

New York Titles

Child Custody, Visitation and Support in NY $26.95
File for Divorce in NY $26.95
How to Form a Corporation in NY (3E) $21.95
How to Make a NY Will (3E) $16.95
How to Start a Business in NY (2E) $18.95
How to Win in Small Claims Court in NY (2E) $18.95
Landlords' Legal Guide in NY $24.95
Tenants' Rights in NY $21.95

North Carolina and South Carolina Titles

How to File for Divorce in NC (3E) $22.95
How to Make a NC Will (3E) $16.95
How to Start a Business in NC or SC $24.95
Landlords' Rights & Duties in NC $21.95

Ohio Titles

How to File for Divorce in OH (3E) $24.95
How to Form a Corporation in OH $24.95
How to Make an OH Will $16.95

Pennsylvania Titles

Child Custody, Visitation and Support in PA $26.95
How to File for Divorce in PA (3E) $26.95
How to Form a Corporation in PA $24.95
How to Make a PA Will (2E) $16.95
How to Start a Business in PA (3E) $21.95
The Landlord's Legal Guide in PA $24.95

Texas Titles

Child Custody, Visitation and Support in TX $22.95
How to File for Divorce in TX (4E) $24.95
How to Form a Corporation in TX (3E) $24.95
How to Make a TX Will (3E) $16.95
How to Probate and Settle an Estate in TX (4E) $26.95
How to Start a Business in TX (4E) $21.95
How to Win in Small Claims Court in TX (2E) $16.95
The Landlord's Legal Guide in TX $24.95

SPHINX® PUBLISHING ORDER FORM

BILL TO:		SHIP TO:	
Phone #	Terms	F.O.B. Chicago, IL	Ship Date

Charge my: ☐ VISA ☐ MasterCard ☐ American Express

☐ **Money Order or Personal Check**

Credit Card Number

Expiration Date

Qty	ISBN	Title	Retail	Ext.	Qty	ISBN	Title	Retail	Ext.
		SPHINX PUBLISHING NATIONAL TITLES				1-57248-156-0	How to Write Your Own Premarital Agreement (3E)	$24.95	
	1-57248-363-6	101 Complaint Letters That Get Results	$18.95			1-57248-230-3	Incorporate in Delaware from Any State	$26.95	
	1-57248-361-X	The 529 College Savings Plan (2E)	$18.95			1-57248-158-7	Incorporate in Nevada from Any State	$24.95	
	1-57248-483-7	The 529 College Savings Plan Made Simple	$7.95			1-57248-474-8	Inmigración a los EE.UU. Paso a Paso (2E)	$24.95	
	1-57248-460-8	The Alternative Minimum Tax	$14.95			1-57248-400-4	Inmigración y Ciudadanía en los EE.UU. Preguntas y Respuestas	$16.95	
	1-57248-349-0	The Antique and Art Collector's Legal Guide	$24.95			1-57248-453-5	Law 101	$16.95	
	1-57248-347-4	Attorney Responsibilities & Client Rights	$19.95			1-57248-374-1	Law School 101	$16.95	
	1-57248-382-2	Child Support	$18.95			1-57248-377-6	The Law (In Plain English)® for Small Business	$19.95	
	1-57248-487-X	Cómo Comprar su Primera Casa	$8.95			1-57248-223-0	Legal Research Made Easy (3E)	$21.95	
	1-57248-148-X	Cómo Hacer su Propio Testamento	$16.95			1-57248-449-7	The Living Trust Kit	$21.95	
	1-57248-462-4	Cómo Negociar su Crédito	$8.95			1-57248-165-X	Living Trusts and Other Ways to Avoid Probate (3E)	$24.95	
	1-57248-463-2	Cómo Organizar un Presupuesto	$8.95			1-57248-186-2	Manual de Beneficios para el Seguro Social	$18.95	
	1-57248-147-1	Cómo Solicitar su Propio Divorcio	$24.95			1-57248-220-6	Mastering the MBE	$16.95	
	1-57248-373-3	The Complete Adoption and Fertility Legal Guide	$24.95			1-57248-455-1	Minding Her Own Business, 4E	$14.95	
	1-57248-166-8	The Complete Book of Corporate Forms	$24.95			1-57248-167-6	Most Val. Business Legal Forms You'll Ever Need (3E)	$21.95	
	1-57248-383-0	The Complete Book of Insurance	$18.95			1-57248-360-1	Most Val. Personal Legal Forms You'll Ever Need (2E)	$26.95	
	1-57248-458-6	The Complete Hiring and Firing Handbook	$18.95			1-57248-388-1	The Power of Attorney Handbook (5E)	$22.95	
	1-57248-353-9	The Complete Kit to Selling Your Own Home	$18.95			1-57248-332-6	Profit from Intellectual Property	$28.95	
	1-57248-229-X	The Complete Legal Guide to Senior Care	$21.95			1-57248-329-6	Protect Your Patent	$24.95	
	1-57248-391-1	The Complete Partnership Book	$24.95			1-57248-376-8	Nursing Homes and Assisted Living Facilities	$19.95	
	1-57248-201-X	The Complete Patent Book	$26.95			1-57248-385-7	Quick Cash	$14.95	
	1-57248-369-5	Credit Smart	$18.95			1-57248-344-X	Repair Your Own Credit and Deal with Debt (2E)	$18.95	
	1-57248-163-3	Crime Victim's Guide to Justice (2E)	$21.95			1-57248-350-4	El Seguro Social Preguntas y Respuestas	$16.95	
	1-57248-367-9	Employees' Rights	$18.95			1-572483865	Seniors' Rights	$19.95	
	1-57248-365-2	Employer's Rights	$24.95			1-57248-217-6	Sexual Harassment: Your Guide to Legal Action	$18.95	
	1-57248-251-6	The Entrepreneur's Internet Handbook	$21.95			1-57248-378-4	Sisters-in-Law	$16.95	
	1-57248-235-4	The Entrepreneur's Legal Guide	$26.95			1-57248-219-2	The Small Business Owner's Guide to Bankruptcy	$21.95	
	1-57248-346-6	Essential Guide to Real Estate Contracts (2E)	$18.95			1-57248-395-4	The Social Security Benefits Handbook (4E)	$18.95	
	1-57248-160-9	Essential Guide to Real Estate Leases	$18.95			1-57248-216-8	Social Security Q&A	$12.95	
	1-57248-375-X	Fathers' Rights	$19.95			1-57248-328-8	Starting Out or Starting Over	$14.95	
	1-57248-450-0	Financing Your Small Business	$17.95			1-57248-221-4	Teen Rights	$22.95	
	1-57248-459-4	Fired, Laid Off or Forced Out	$14.95			1-57248-457-8	Tax Power for the Self-Employed	$17.95	
	1-57248-502-7	The Frequent Traveler's Guide	$14.95			1-57248-366-0	Tax Smarts for Small Business	$21.95	
	1-57248-331-8	Gay & Lesbian Rights	$26.95			1-57248-236-2	Unmarried Parents' Rights (2E)	$19.95	
	1-57248-139-0	Grandparents' Rights (3E)	$24.95			1-57248-362-8	U.S. Immigration and Citizenship Q&A	$18.95	
	1-57248-475-6	Guía de Inmigración a Estados Unidos (4E)	$24.95			1-57248-387-3	U.S. Immigration Step by Step (2E)	$24.95	
	1-57248-187-0	Guía de Justicia para Victimas del Crimen	$21.95			1-57248-392-X	U.S.A. Immigration Guide (5E)	$26.95	
	1-57248-253-2	Guía Esencial para los Contratos de Arrendamiento de Bienes Raices	$22.95			1-57248-451-9	What to Do — Before "I DO"	$14.95	
	1-57248-334-2	Homeowner's Rights	$19.95			1-57248-225-7	Win Your Unemployment Compensation Claim (2E)	$21.95	
	1-57248-164-1	How to Buy a Condominium or Townhome (2E)	$19.95			1-57248-330-X	The Wills, Estate Planning and Trusts Legal Kit	$26.95	
	1-57248-328-8	How to Buy Your First Home	$18.95			1-57248-473-X	Winning Your Personal Injury Claim (3E)	$24.95	
	1-57248-384-9	How to Buy a Franchise	$19.95			1-57248-333-4	Working with Your Homeowners Association	$19.95	
	1-57248-472-1	How to File Your Own Bankruptcy (6E)	$21.95			1-57248-380-6	Your Right to Child Custody, Visitation and Support (3E)	$24.95	
	1-57248-343-1	How to File Your Own Divorce (5E)	$26.95						
	1-57248-222-2	How to Form a Limited Liability Company (2E)	$24.95						
	1-57248-390-3	How to Form a Nonprofit Corporation (3E)	$24.95						
	1-57248-345-8	How to Form Your Own Corporation (4E)	$26.95						
	1-57248-232-X	How to Make Your Own Simple Will (3E)	$18.95						
	1-57248-379-2	How to Register Your Own Copyright (5E)	$24.95						
	1-57248-394-6	How to Write Your Own Living Will (4E)	$18.95				**Total for this page**		

To order, call Sourcebooks at 1-800-432-7444 or FAX (630) 961-2168 (Bookstores, libraries, wholesalers—please call for discount)
Prices are subject to change without notice.
Find more legal information at: **www.SphinxLegal.com**

SPHINX® PUBLISHING ORDER FORM

Qty	ISBN	Title	Retail	Ext.
		CALIFORNIA TITLES		
____	1-57248-337-7	How to File for Divorce in CA (4E)	$26.95	____
____	1-57248-464-0	How to Settle and Probate an Estate in CA	$28.95	____
____	1-57248-336-9	How to Start a Business in CA (2E)	$21.95	____
____	1-57248-194-3	How to Win in Small Claims Court in CA (2E)	$18.95	____
____	1-57248-246-X	Make Your Own CA Will	$18.95	____
____	1-57248-397-0	The Landlord's Legal Guide in CA (2E)	$24.95	____
____	1-57248-241-9	Tenants' Rights in CA	$21.95	____
		FLORIDA TITLES		
____	1-57248-396-2	How to File for Divorce in FL (8E)	$28.95	____
____	1-57248-356-3	How to Form a Corporation in FL (6E)	$24.95	____
____	1-57248-490-X	How to Form a Limited Liability Co. in FL (3E)	$24.95	____
____	1-57071-401-0	How to Form a Partnership in FL	$22.95	____
____	1-57248-456-X	How to Make a FL Will (7E)	$16.95	____
____	1-57248-354-7	How to Probate and Settle an Estate in FL (5E)	$26.95	____
____	1-57248-339-3	How to Start a Business in FL (7E)	$21.95	____
____	1-57248-204-4	How to Win in Small Claims Court in FL (7E)	$18.95	____
____	1-57248-381-4	Land Trusts in Florida (7E)	$29.95	____
____	1-57248-338-5	Landlords' Rights and Duties in FL (9E)	$22.95	____
		GEORGIA TITLES		
____	1-57248-340-7	How to File for Divorce in GA (5E)	$21.95	____
____	1-57248-180-3	How to Make a GA Will (4E)	$16.95	____
____	1-57248-341-5	How to Start a Business in Georgia (3E)	$21.95	____
		ILLINOIS TITLES		
____	1-57248-244-3	Child Custody, Visitation, and Support in IL	$24.95	____
____	1-57248-206-0	How to File for Divorce in IL (3E)	$24.95	____
____	1-57248-170-6	How to Make an IL Will (3E)	$16.95	____
____	1-57248-265-9	How to Start a Business in IL (4E)	$21.95	____
____	1-57248-252-4	The Landlord's Legal Guide in IL	$24.95	____
		MARYLAND, VIRGINIA AND THE DISTRICT OF COLUMBIA		
____	1-57248-240-0	How to File for Divorce in MD, VA and DC	$28.95	____
____	1-57248-359-8	How to Start a Business in MD, VA or DC	$21.95	____
		MASSACHUSETTS TITLES		
____	1-57248-115-3	How to Form a Corporation in MA	$24.95	____
____	1-57248-466-7	How to Start a Business in MA (4E)	$21.95	____
____	1-57248-398-9	The Landlord's Legal Guide in MA (2E)	$24.95	____
		MICHIGAN TITLES		
____	1-57248-467-5	How to File for Divorce in MI (4E)	$24.95	____
____	1-57248-182-X	How to Make a MI Will (3E)	$16.95	____
____	1-57248-183-8	How to Start a Business in MI (3E)	$18.95	____
		MINNESOTA TITLES		
____	1-57248-142-0	How to File for Divorce in MN	$21.95	____
____	1-57248-179-X	How to Form a Corporation in MN	$24.95	____
____	1-57248-178-1	How to Make a MN Will (2E)	$16.95	____
		NEW JERSEY TITLES		
____	1-57248-239-7	How to File for Divorce in NJ	$24.95	____
____	1-57248-448-9	How to Start a Business in NJ	$21.95	____
		NEW YORK TITLES		
____	1-57248-193-5	Child Custody, Visitation and Support in NY	$26.95	____
____	1-57248-351-2	File for Divorce in NY	$26.95	____
____	1-57248-249-4	How to Form a Corporation in NY (2E)	$24.95	____
____	1-57248-401-2	How to Make a NY Will (3E)	$16.95	____
____	1-57248-469-1	How to Start a Business in NY (3E)	$21.95	____
____	1-57248-198-6	How to Win in Small Claims Court in NY (2E)	$18.95	____
____	1-57248-122-6	Tenants' Rights in NY	$21.95	____

Qty	ISBN	Title	Retail	Ext.
		NORTH CAROLINA TITLES		
____	1-57248-185-4	How to File for Divorce in NC (3E)	$22.95	____
____	1-57248-184-6	How to Start a Business in NC (3E)	$18.95	____
____	1-57248-091-2	Landlords' Rights & Duties in NC	$21.95	____
		NORTH CAROLINA AND SOUTH CAROLINA TITLES		
____	1-57248-371-7	How to Start a Business in NC or SC	$24.95	____
		OHIO TITLES		
____	1-57248-503-5	How to File for Divorce in OH (3E)	$24.95	____
____	1-57248-174-9	How to Form a Corporation in OH	$24.95	____
____	1-57248-173-0	How to Make an OH Will	$16.95	____
		PENNSYLVANIA TITLES		
____	1-57248-242-7	Child Custody, Visitation and Support in PA	$26.95	____
____	1-57248-211-7	How to File for Divorce in PA (3E)	$26.95	____
____	1-57248-358-X	How to Form a Cooporation in PA	$24.95	____
____	1-57248-094-7	How to Make a PA Will (2E)	$16.95	____
____	1-57248-357-1	How to Start a Business in PA (3E)	$21.95	____
____	1-57248-245-1	The Landlord's Legal Guide in PA	$24.95	____
		TEXAS TITLES		
____	1-57248-171-4	Child Custody, Visitation, and Support in TX	$22.95	____
____	1-57248-399-7	How to File for Divorce in TX (4E)	$24.95	____
____	1-57248-470-5	How to Form a Corporation in TX (3E)	$24.95	____
____	1-57248-255-9	How to Make a TX Will (3E)	$16.95	____
____	1-57248-496-9	How to Probate and Settle an Estate in TX (4E)	$26.95	____
____	1-57248-471-3	How to Start a Business in TX (4E)	$21.95	____
____	1-57248-355-5	The Landlord's Legal Guide in TX	$24.95	____

SubTotal This page ____

SubTotal previous page ____

Shipping— $5.00 for 1st book, $1.00 each additional ____

Illinois residents add 6.75% sales tax ____

Connecticut residents add 6.00% sales tax ____

Total ____

To order, call Sourcebooks at 1-800-432-7444 or FAX (630) 961-2168 (Bookstores, libraries, wholesalers—please call for discount)

Prices are subject to change without notice.

Find more legal information at: www.SphinxLegal.com

How to Use the CD-ROM

Thank you for purchasing *The Weekend Landlord*. We have worked hard to put together exactly what you need to get started as a landlord and to make sure that you are aware of some of the legal ramifications involved in your endeavor. We have also gathered what we believe to be some of the most important forms and documents you need to be successful. To make this material even more useful, we have included every document found in Appendix J on a CD-ROM that is attached to the inside back cover of the book.

Use the list at the end of this section for help finding the form you are looking for. You can use these forms just as you would the forms in the book. Print them out, fill them in, and use them however you need. You can also fill in the forms directly on your computer. Just identify the form you need, open it, click on the space where the information should go, and input your information. Customize each form for your particular needs. Use them over and over again.

The CD-ROM is compatible with both PC and Mac operating systems. (While it should work with either operating system, we cannot guarantee that it will work with your particular system and we cannot provide technical assistance.) To use the forms on your computer, you will need to use Acrobat® Reader®. The CD-ROM does not contain this program. You can download this program from Adobe's website at **www.adobe.com**. Click on the "Get Acrobat® Reader®" icon to begin the download process and follow the instructions.

Once you have Acrobat® Reader® installed, insert the CD-ROM into your computer. Double click on the icon representing the disc on your desktop or go through your hard drive to identify the drive that contains the disc and click on it.

Once opened, you will see the files contained on the CD-ROM listed as "Form #: [Form Title]." Open the file you need through Acrobat® Reader®. You may print the form to fill it out manually at this point, or your can use the "Hand Tool" and click on the appropriate line to fill it in using your computer.

Any time you see bracketed information [ ] on the form, you can click on it and delete the bracketed information from your final form. This information is only a reference guide to assist you in filling in the forms and should be removed from your final version. Once all your information is filled in, you can print your filled-in form.

NOTE: *Acrobat® Reader® does not allow you to save the PDF with the boxes filled in.*

. . . .

Purchasers of this book are granted a license to use the forms contained in it for their own personal use. By purchasing this book, you have also purchased a limited license to use all forms on the accompanying CD-ROM. The license limits you to personal use only and all other copyright laws must be adhered. No claim of copyright is made in any government form reproduced in the book or on the CD-ROM. You are free to modify the forms and tailor them to your specific situation.

The author and publisher have attempted to provide the most current and up-to-date information available. However, the courts, Congress, and your state's legislatures review, modify, and change laws on an ongoing basis, as well as create new laws from time to time. By the very nature of the information and due to the continual changes in our legal system, to be sure that you have the current and best information for your situation, you should consult a local attorney or research the current laws yourself.

. . . .

This publication is designed to provide accurate and authoritative information in regard to the subject matter covered. It is sold with the understanding that the publisher is not engaged in rendering legal, accounting, or other professional service. If legal advice or other expert assistance is required, the services of a competent professional person should be sought.

> *—From a Declaration of Principles Jointly Adopted by a Committee of the American Bar Association and a Committee of Publishers and Associations*

This product is not a substitute for legal advice.

> *—Disclaimer required by Texas statutes.*